Emery
X934
B-1
G. Sl,

Periodicals on the Socialist Countries and on Marxism

Harry G. Shaffer

The Praeger Special Studies program—utilizing the most modern and efficient book production techniques and a selective worldwide distribution network—makes available to the academic, government, and business communities significant, timely research in U.S. and international economic, social, and political development.

Periodicals on the Socialist Countries and on Marxism

A New Annotated Index of English-Language Publications

Praeger Publishers   New York   Washington   London

PRAEGER SPECIAL STUDIES IN INTERNATIONAL POLITICS AND GOVERNMENT

Library of Congress Cataloging in Publication Data

Shaffer, Harry G
    Periodicals on the socialist countries and on Marxism.

    (Praeger special studies in international politics
and government)
    Edition of 1971 published under title: English language
periodic publications on communism.
    Bibliography
    Includes indexes.
    1. Communism—Periodicals—Bibliography. 2. Communist
countries—Periodicals—Bibliography. I. Title.
Z7164.S67S435   1976 [HX3]   016.909'09'717   75-36907
ISBN 0-275-24010-X

The original edition of this index
was published in 1971 by the Research Institute
on Communist Affairs (since 1974, the Research
Institute on International Change), School of
International Affairs, Columbia University.

PRAEGER PUBLISHERS
111 Fourth Avenue, New York, N.Y. 10003, U.S.A.

Published in the United States of America in 1977
by Praeger Publishers, Inc.

Printed in the United States of America

To my children—Bernie, Ron, Lennie and
Tanya

and to Debbie

The 16 countries covered in this index have often been referred to as "Communist" countries in the West. Since none of them lays claim to having reached a "final stage of communism," they call themselves "socialist" countries. This term has been used increasingly by Western scholars in the field and lately also by U.S. government agencies, such as the Department of Commerce, and they are also referred to as "socialist" countries throughout this index. The social order of these countries is broadly characterized by the paramount position of a single leadership party, by strict adherence to Marxist or Marxist-Leninist ideology as interpreted and espoused by that party and its leadership, by the social ownership of most of the means of production, and by central economic command planning. Of the 16, only Yugoslavia does not quite fit this description. Listed by the U.S. Department of Commerce among "Western" nations, it is included here partly for historical reasons and partly because the country's ideological orientation and its unique economic and political system are of great interest to many Western scholars who specialize in Slavic and Soviet area studies and in the study of Marxism per se.

In alphabetical order, the 16 countries included in this index are as follows:

Name generally used in this index	Country's official name
Albania	People's Republic of Albania
Bulgaria	People's Republic of Bulgaria
Cambodia	Democratic Kampuchea
China	People's Republic of China
Cuba	Republic of Cuba
Czechoslovakia	Socialist Republic of Czechoslovakia
GDR	German Democratic Republic
Hungary	Hungarian People's Republic
Laos	Lao Democratic Republic
Mongolia	Mongolian People's Republic
North Korea	Democratic People's Republic of Korea
Poland	Polish People's Republic
Romania	Socialist Republic of Romania
USSR (Soviet Union)	Union of Soviet Socialist Republics

Name generally used in this index	Country's official name
Vietnam	Socialist Republic of Vietnam
Yugoslavia	Federal Socialist Republic of Yugoslavia

As used in this index, then, "socialist" countries refers only to the 16 listed above and not to others, such as Algeria, Tanzania, or Mozambique, which see their economic, political, and social structure as basically socialist in nature, or to Western countries in which a democratically elected, moderately socialist political party is in power.

Articles on Marxism, on Marxism-Leninism, on communism, or on one or another of the socialist countries can be found in countless English-language periodicals—popular, semischolarly, and scientific. Included in this index are only those periodicals that concentrate on subject matter of concern to students of communism whose interest lies in the social sciences, in the humanities, or in related fields. Omitted, therefore, are periodicals that deal with technical subjects of interest only to specialists in other fields, such as Soviet Radio Chemistry, the Chinese Medical Journal, or the Hungarian Journal of Thermal Analysis. Also omitted are the annual statistical yearbooks and statistical pocketbooks published in English, or in their languages with English translations of the table headings, by most of the socialist countries and surely by all the socialist countries in East Europe. (Interested researchers should address inquiries to the respective country's Central Statistical Administration in its capital or to the country's embassy in Washington, D.C., or in London.) Omitted, too, are most periodic publications that are not primarily devoted to Communist studies, such as the New York Times, Fortune, Harper's, the Harvard Business Review, the American Economic Review, and the American Political Science Review. And also omitted are the many periodic publications that, while concerned with communism, deal primarily with one nonsocialist country, such as the pro-Communist British Labour Monthly or the anti-Communist U.S. American Opinion.

There are numerous other periodicals, such as The Communist, Revolution, Worker's Press, or Science for the People, published by Trotskyist groups, by the "New Left," and by other radical left-wing organizations in the United States and elsewhere. Most of these have also been omitted, since their inclusion would make this index too unwieldy and since, so far at least, they are not used extensively by Western scholars concerned with understanding Marxism-Leninism or with analyzing developments in socialist countries. However, the

Fourth International, as the official voice of the world Trotskyist movement, has been incorporated into this index.

Some of those who use this index will understandably feel that certain periodicals that have been consciously omitted belong in it while others that have been included do not. Admittedly, the decision in borderline cases was not always easy. In general, the following basic criterion was used in such instances: If it was felt that the journal under consideration could contribute to a better understanding of the ideological framework, the culture, or the economic, political, and social structure of one or more of the socialist countries, or to a better understanding of Marxist ideology as such, it was included; if not, it was omitted. So, for instance, Hungarian Heavy Industries was included, since it contains many nontechnical articles that focus on economic aspects of these industries and on their impact on the Hungarian economy; but Czechoslovak Heavy Industry was not, because it is a very technical journal, of interest probably only to engineers and technicians. Asian Quarterly and Asian Outlook were included, since many of their articles deal with socialist countries in Asia; but Southeast Asia was not, because it concentrates with but rare exceptions on nonsocialist countries in the region. For the same reason, the United Nations' Economic Bulletin for Europe was included, but its Economic Bulletin for Asia and the Pacific was not; and publications issuing from South Korea or from Taiwan were included only if they regularly devote editorials, commentaries, and articles to North Korea or mainland China, respectively. Or, to give another example, the official organ of the Communist party of Great Britain, Marxism Today, and the U.S. Communist party's Political Affairs were included, since they regularly feature articles on Marxist-Leninist ideology, usually as interpreted in the USSR, as well as articles on socialist countries; but the U.S. Communist party's Daily World was not, since it focuses almost exclusively on Western capitalist countries and especially on the United States.

In collecting material for this index, I made extensive use of the libraries at the University of Kansas and the University of California at Berkeley and of the New York Public Library; I went through numerous specialized bookstores in New York and San Francisco; I made personal visits to such representative agencies as the Soviet Embassy in Washington, D.C., and the Romanian Library and the Yugoslav Press and Cultural Center in New York; I sent off hundreds of letters of inquiry to periodical publishers, editors, and agents in countries around the world, to U.S., British, and Canadian embassies in the socialist countries, and to the embassies of the socialist countries in Washington, D.C., London, and Ottawa. I am immensely grateful for the extensive cooperation I encountered almost everywhere. Without it, this index could not have been compiled.

For each periodical included in this index, as much of the following information as could be secured has been furnished:

1. Title. The articles a, an, and the have been left out at the beginning of a periodical's title. Where there is more than one periodical by the same name included in this index, the place of publication is given in parentheses after the title—the city if it is published in New York or in a nation's capital, the country otherwise.

2. Contents. A brief description is supplied, especially of the primary focus of the periodical, without making any attempt to pass judgment on the periodical's worthiness in terms of scholarliness, reliability, literary merits, or otherwise.

3. Declared purpose. The publisher's declared purpose or description is supplied only where it helps the reader to get a better picture of the periodical's slant and focus.

4. Special sections. Chronologies of events, book reviews, letters to the editor, and other special sections are enumerated if they seem to be regular features of the periodical.

5. Sample titles. Usually three representative titles of recent articles are supplied.

6. Number of pages. Where the number of pages varies, an approximate, average, or maximum and minimum number of pages per issue is given.

7. Frequency of publication. Since the word bimonthly is ambiguous (it can mean twice a month or every other month), the terms "every two weeks," "twice a month," or "every two months" are used.

8. Publisher. The title of the publication organization, where it is different from the title of the periodical, and full address are given.

9. "Obtainable from . . ." Wherever subscriptions are handled not by the publisher but by a separate agency, the agency's name and address are furnished. Subscriptions to periodicals that issue from the socialist countries are usually accepted by many specialized bookstores and agents in the United States. For a partial listing of these, see pp. 132-34. In the index itself, the address is given in each case only of the agency in the socialist country from which subscriptions can be ordered directly.

10. Subscription price. Subscription prices are for the United States and, unless otherwise stated, are in U.S. dollars per year. Some publishers give subscription rates in their country's currency only; these are listed in the index as given. Because of fluctuating

exchange rates, no attempt has been made to translate them into U.S. dollars.

11. Marxist or non-Marxist. Each periodical is identified as (M), (N/M), (M; N/M), or (U). (M) stands for Marxist. Under this designation fall all periodicals published in any of the 16 socialist countries, Western translations of materials published in the socialist countries (irrespective of the ideological orientation of the translating agency, which could be strongly anti-Communist), and periodic publications by individuals, groups, organizations, and agencies outside the socialist countries which consider themselves Marxist, as this term would generally be interpreted in at least one of the socialist countries—the Fourth International being the only major exception. (N/M) stands for non-Marxist, which, it should be noted, does not necessarily mean anti-Marxist. This designation is used for periodicals that contain very little or no material such as would be included in those identified as (M). The designation (M; N/M) is reserved for periodic publications that regularly feature original or translated articles by Marxists as well as others by non-Marxist contributors. For instance, the Journal of Croatian Studies, published by the Croatian Academy of America, is surely non-Marxist. But since in addition to non-Marxist material it also carries translations of Yugoslav documents and translations of articles and poems published originally in present-day Croatia, it is identified as (M; N/M). (U) stands for unclassified and is used in the cases of the few periodicals where the designation of Marxist or non-Marxist could not be made with any degree of certainty—usually because I was not able to secure a copy of the periodical and did not receive a reply to my inquiry. No further subdividion (pro-Chinese, pro-Soviet, Western independent Marxist, scientific, semiscientific, popular) has been attempted, and the reader is warned not to expect homogeneity either in ideological orientation or in scientific value among the journals in either of the two major divisions. Conclusions as to more precise ideological orientation can often be drawn either from the title, the place of publication, or the description of the periodical.

12. "Since . . ." The year when publication of the periodical was started is supplied.

Where any of the above information is missing, the reader may assume that I have been unable to obtain it. In the case of a handful of periodicals, only minimal information, such as title, address, and subscription price, are furnished, and these periodicals have been marked "(No further information procured.)." These are the cases in which I have been unable to get hold of a copy of the periodical and letters of inquiry to the publisher have remained unanswered, or the periodical was discovered or started publishing when this index started to go to press, too late for further inquiries.

A geographic reference index has been appended to the end of the annotated alphabetical index to enable researchers working on one specific country or region to find readily the periodic publications applicable to their study. In the geographic index, each of the 16 socialist countries is listed, and each periodic publication is included according to its major orientation: For instance, a journal published in Belgrade that concentrates on the Yugoslav economy but has an occasional article on the economy of another socialist country is included under Yugoslavia only. Some journals, however, are listed under more than one country (for instance, those dealing with the Balkan region). To accommodate somewhat more general periodicals, the geographic reference index also has subdivisions titled "General," "Asia," and "East Europe."

I want to take this opportunity to thank once again the many publishers, editors, agencies, book stores, and librarians who helped me so much in collecting the necessary information. Last, but by no means least, I want to express my special gratitude to Deborah Spector, who, as my assistant on the project, was of substantial aid in all stages of the preparation of this index.

CONTENTS

Periodicals on the Socialist Countries and on Marxism

AAASS Newsletter. Professional news items for members of the American Association for the Advancement of Slavic Studies (AAASS), the national organization for scholars working in the field of Slavic and Soviet area studies. Reports on fellowships, awards, grants; calendar of conferences; news of the association and of regional affiliates; university appointments and staff changes; quarterly "Bulletin from the International Research and Exchanges Board"; quarterly "news from the Kennan Center for Advanced Russian Studies"; other items of special professional interest to AAASS members. 12 pages per issue. Published eight times per year by the American Association for the Advancement of Slavic Studies, 190 West 19th Avenue, Room 254, Ohio State University, Columbus, Ohio 43210. Free to AAASS members, who also receive the Slavic Review and the Directory of Members (for membership dues, see Slavic Review); $5.00 per year for nonmembers. (N/M) Since 1960.

ABN Correspondence. Focus on alleged oppression in socialist countries, especially in the Soviet Union and East Europe, and on alleged Communist subversive activities in nonsocialist countries. Reports on conferences; book reviews; letters to the editor; some pictures. Sample titles of recent articles: "Estonians and Georgians in Russian Concentration Camps," "Communist Military Threat and National Liberation," "Intensified Persecution of Christians in the CSSR." 48 pages per issue. Published every two months by the Press Bureau of the Anti-Bolshevik Block of Nations (ABN), Zeppelinstrasse 67, 8 Munich 80, West Germany. $9.00 per year. (N/M) Since 1973.

ABSEES. Abstracts of books, newspapers, and journals published in the USSR and the socialist countries of East Europe. Up to 1,000 entries per issue. Occasional specialized bibliographies (a recent one, for instance, entitled Prague Spring and "Normalization": A Selected Bibliography of Czechoslovak Books from 1968-74). Subscribers also receive, twice a year, an Information Bulletin on British and international developments in the field of Soviet and East European studies; also an Annual Bibliography of British Writings on the U.S.S.R. and Eastern Europe, which draws on over 150 periodicals published in the United Kingdom and includes

also relevant books and book reviews. Published quarterly by the
Institute of Soviet and East European Studies of the University of
Glasgow, Glasgow, G12 8QG, Scotland. $36.00 per year; joint sub-
scription to ABSEES (Abstracts, Soviet and East European Series)
and Soviet Studies (see below), at concessionary joint rate (was
$45.00 per year in 1976). Special joint rate for NASEES (National
Association for Soviet and East European Studies) members and
bona fide students (was $21.00 per year in 1976). (M; N/M) Since
1970.

Abstracts of Bulgarian Scientific Literature: Economics and Law. Abstracts of articles on economics and law originally published in
Bulgarian periodic publications, documents, and books. Section
on economics in English; section on law in French. Economics
section subdivided into "Economics of Socialism" (which includes
problems of Bulgaria's socialist economy), "Economics of Capitalism," "Economic History," and "Economy of the Developing Countries." Sample titles of recent articles in economics section: "Population and Manpower," "The Role of Planning in the Effective Use
of Resources," "Profitability of Agricultural Production in the
People's Republic of Bulgaria." 24 to 40 pages per issue (of which
about two-thirds are on economics and one-third on law). Published quarterly by the Scientific Information Centre for Natural,
Mathematical and Social Sciences at the Bulgarian Academy of
Sciences, 1, 7 Noemvri Street, Sofia, Bulgaria. $4.20 per year.
(M) Since 1958.

Abstracts of Hungarian Economic Literature. Abstracts of books and
articles on economic matters and related topics, most of them
published in Hungary, by Hungarian authors. Abstracts are usually
1 to 6 pages in length. Sample titles of recently abstracted books
and articles: Modernization of Production and Economic Growth,
"Hungarian Price Policy and Capitalist Inflation," What Should be
Known About the Common Market. Length varies from under 200
to well over 300 pages per issue. Published every two months by
the Scientific Information Service of the Hungarian Scientific Council for World Economy, Editorial Office, P.O. Box 36, H-1531
Budapest, Hungary. Obtainable from Kultura, P.O. Box 149,
H-1389 Budapest 62, Hungary. $18.00 per year. (M) Since 1971.

ACES Bulletin (successor to ASTE Bulletin). Articles on comparative
economics, economic systems, and economic planning and development. Strong emphasis on socialist economies and especially on
the Soviet Union and the socialist countries of East Europe. Announcements; notes; book reviews. Sample titles of recent articles:
"Soviet Economic Concessions: The Agony and the Promise,"

"US-Romanian Trade Relations," "Urban and Social Economics in
Market and Planned Economies." Averages about 90 pages per
issue. Published three times per year at the International Development Research Center, Indiana University, Bloomington, Indiana
47401. Free to members of the Association for Comparative Economic Studies (ACES). Membership dues: $3.75 per year for stu-
dents, $7.50 for regular members, and $15.00 for institutional
memberships. (M; N/M) (The ACES Bulletin is being replaced, as
of January 1, 1977, by the Journal of Comparative Economics.
The latter is not yet available as this index goes to press.)

Acta Historiae Artium. Papers on the history of the arts. Text in
English, French, Italian, German, and Russian. Published quar-
terly by the Hungarian Academy of Sciences, P.O. Box 24, H-1363
Budapest 502, Hungary. Obtainable from Kultura, P.O. Box 149,
H-1389 Budapest 62, Hungary. $40.00 per year. (M) Since 1953.

Acta Historica. Emphasis on historical problems as they relate to
Hungary. Book reviews. Some articles in English, others in
French, Russian, or German. Sample titles of recent English-
language articles: "East-Central Europe and World War II," "Ways
and Peculiarities of Enterprise Development in the 20th Century
Hungarian Industry," "The Nature of the Revolution Subsequent to
the Liberation in Hungary and the Principal Issues of the Policy of
the Communist Party." About 200 to 250 pages per issue. Pub-
lished twice a year by the Hungarian Academy of Sciences, P.O.
Box 24, H-1363 Budapest 502, Hungary. Obtainable from Kultura,
P.O. Box 147, H-1389 Budapest 62, Hungary. $32.00 per year.
(M) Since 1951.

Acta Litteraria. Emphasis on comparative literature. Declared purpose: to deal "with problems in Hungarian and East European history of literature . . . stress is laid on the relation between Hungarian literature and literatures of other European countries in
the past . . . as well as on the place and role of Hungarian letters
in world literature. The latest results achieved by Hungarian
scholars are reviewed." Book reviews. Some articles in English,
others in other major languages. Sample titles of recent English-
language articles: "World Literature and the Comparative Analysis
of Literature," "Edgar Allen Poe in Russia," "Russian Studies of
American Literature." 200 to 250 pages per issue. Published
twice a year by the Hungarian Academy of Sciences, P.O. Box 24,
H-1363 Budapest 502, Hungary. Obtainable from Kultura, P.O.
Box 149, H-1389 Budapest 62, Hungary. $32.00 per year. (M)

Acta Oeconomica. Emphasis on economic theory and on economic
conditions, developments, and problems in Hungary. Most articles
in English, some in Russian. Book reviews. Sample titles of recent articles: "Macrofunctions Computed on the Basis of Plan Mod-
els," "The Complex Program of the CMEA and the Possibilities
of Economic Cooperation with West-European Countries," "The
Situation and Role of Private Small-Scale Industry in Hungary."
Published eight times per year, making up two volumes of some
400 pages each, by the Publishing House of the Hungarian Academy
of Sciences, Budapest, Hungary. Obtainable from Kultura, P.O.
Box 149, H-1389 Budapest 62, Hungary. $32.00 per year. (M)
Since 1966.

Acta Poloniae Historica. Articles on ancient, medieval, modern,
and contemporary history. Some emphasis on present-day Poland.
Most articles in English, some in French and German. Sample
titles of recent English-language articles: "Creative Processes of
the Formation of Socialist Society in Poland (1944-1974)," "The
Foreign Policy of People's Poland in the Past Thirty Years,"
"General Regularities and Specific Features of the Building of
Socialism in Poland (1944-1948)." Averages about 330 pages per
issue. Published twice a year by the Committee for Historical
Science, Institute of History, Polish Academy of Sciences, Warsaw, Poland. Obtainable from Ruch, P.O. Box 154, ul. Wronia
23, Warsaw, Poland. $5.65 per issue. (M)

African Communist. Articles on ideology; on current political and
economic conditions, problems, and developments in South Africa;
on its Communist movement; and on socialism and communism
elsewhere in the world. Declared purpose: "Published . . . in the
interest of African solidarity and as a forum for Marxist-Leninist
thought throughout our [the African] continent." Book reviews;
documents. Sample titles of recent articles: "Socialist Humanism
vs. Racist Inhumanity," "Women's Role in the South African Freedom Fight," "How Czechoslovakia Solves the Nationalities Question." Published quarterly by the South African Communist party.
Obtainable from Inkululeko Publications, 39 Goodge Street, London W1, England. $4.00 per year; $10.00 by airmail. (M) Since
1959.

Agricultural Literature of Czechoslovakia. One-paragraph abstracts,
in English translation, of articles on agriculture originally published in Czechoslovak journals. Subdivided into such sections as
"Agricultural Economics," "Plant Production," "Livestock Production," "Veterinary Medicine," and "Forestry" (including hunt-

ing). Sample titles of recent articles abstracted: "Macroeconomic
Characteristics of Prognosis in Agriculture," "A Study of the Possibilities of the Endogenous Control of Tillering in Winter Wheat,"
"The Toxicity of Pesticides on the Basis of Chlorinated Hydrocar-
bons and Phenols and Their Proof in Fish." Averages around 130
pages (close to 500 abstracts) per issue. Published twice a year
by the Institute for Scientific and Technical Information, Ministry
of Agriculture, Forestry and Water Management, Slezska 7, 12056
Prague 2, Czechoslovakia. Available on exchange basis only. (M)
Since 1956.

AIMS Newsletter. Information, announcements (including announcements of forthcoming conferences), and bibliographies of significant books, pamphlets, periodical articles, unpublished dissertations, and archival accessions of interest primarily to students of
Marxism and of Marxist analysis of economic, social, political,
cultural, and historical issues. Bibliographies list both Marxist
and non-Marxist items. Eight pages per issue. Published every
two months by the American Institute for Marxist Studies (AIMS),
20 East 30th Street, New York, N.Y. 10016. $5.00 per year.
(M) Since 1964.

AIMS Publications Series. Four series of publications of interest to
students of Marxism and of Marxist analysis of economic, social,
political, cultural, and historical issues. The four series are
"Monograph Series" (sample title: Marxism and Democracy);
"Historical Series" (sample title: Robert Owen in the United States);
"Occasional Papers" (sample title: Humanistic Philosophy in Contemporary Poland and Yugoslavia); and "Bibliographies" (sample
title: U.S. Intervention in Latin America: An Annotated Bibliography). Items vary in length from 40 to 400 pages; some are authored
by Marxists, others by non-Marxists sympathetic to socialist
ideas. Published irregularly by the American Institute for Marxist
Studies (AIMS), 20 East 30th Street, New York, N.Y. 10016.
Prices per item vary, depending upon length and whether paper-
bound or clothbound, from 60 cents to $10.00. Complete list and
prices of all titles available on request. (M; N/M)

Albania Report. Emphasis on ideology, on various aspects of life in
Albania, and on progress of communism elsewhere in the world.
About one half of each issue devoted to one main theme, such as
"Historical Development of Albanian Agriculture," "People's As-
sembly Adopts State Budget and Economic Plan for 1975," "Joyful
Celebration of 30th Anniversary of Liberation." Individual articles
are short, mostly one to three paragraphs. Sample titles of recent

articles: "Art Should Reflect Socialist Reality," "New Tirana-
Peking Airline Inaugurated," "Developing Countries Stand Up."
Four pages per issue. Published every two months under the ed-
itorship of the Albania Affairs Study Group by Albania Report,
P.O. Box 912, New York, N.Y. 10008. $3.00 per year. (M)
Since 1970.

Albania Today. Emphasis on ideology and on various aspects of life
in Albania. Some pictures. Review of Albanian press. Sample
titles of recent articles: "On the Class Struggle in Socialism,"
"Torch Bearer of Albanian Culture," "A Free Woman Can Live
Only in a Free Society." About 64 pages per issue. Published
every two months in Tirana, Albania. Obtainable from "Ndermarja
e Librit," Tirana, Albania. $3.60 per year. (M) Since 1971.

Albanian Resistance. News bulletin with emphasis on political and
economic life in Albania as seen through the eyes of Albanian
emigrés. Also reports on activities of Albanians abroad. A recent issue was subdivided into two parts: "News from Enslaved
Albania" and "In Exile." 10 to 14 pages per issue. Published irregularly by the National Democratic Committee for a Free Albania, 18 bis rue Brunel, Paris 17, France (New York office:
204 East 25th Street, New York, N.Y. 10010). Free. (N/M)

American Bibliography of Slavic and East European Studies. Bibliography of books in the area of Russian and East European studies
and of relevant articles taken from books of readings and from
more than 400 journals and magazines. Listings include all relevant material published in the United States and Canada and by
Americans abroad, and selected works in English, published any-
where outside the Soviet Union and East Europe. Omitted are items
that have as their sole place of publication newspapers. This bibliography is divided by discipline (for instance, "Anthropology and
Sociology," "History," "Public Affairs, Law and Government");
each section is subdivided, primarily by country; in some cases,
countries are further subdivided by areas within a discipline. For
instance, "Soviet Union," under "Economics," is subdivided into
"General," "Agriculture," "Industry and Management," "Economic Growth and Development," and "Wages and Prices." Includes
monographs, journal articles, published reports and proceedings,
book reviews, dissertations, and obituaries. Estimate length of
future volumes: about 5,000 entries (the 1974 issue had 5,327 entries) and about 200 to 250 pages per issue. Prepared annually at
the U.S. Library of Congress. Obtainable from the American Association for the Advancement of Slavic Studies (AAASS) 190 West

19th Avenue, Room 254, Ohio State University, Columbus, Ohio 43210. Price varies; the Bibliography for 1974, published in 1976, was $12.00; $10.00 for AAASS members. (For membership dues, see Slavic Review) (N/M) Since 1957.

American Bulletin. Critical analysis of political, economic, and social conditions in Czechoslovakia. Occasional articles on events elsewhere of special interest to Czechoslovakians living abroad. Sample titles of recent articles: "Life in Czechoslovakia: The Myth of Communist Progress," " 'We Want Freedom,' " "Czechoslovak Independence Day in Washington." Four pages per issue. Published monthly by the Czechoslovak National Council of America, 2137 South Lombard Avenue, Cicero, Illinois 60650. $2.00 per year; free to members of the Czechoslovak National Council of America (membership dues, $4.00 per year). (N/M)

American Review of East-West Trade. Illustrated magazine devoted to the promotion of East-West trade. Contributions by business leaders, commercial specialists, and government officials, East and West. Ads of products from both Western and socialist countries offered for sale abroad. Described by the publishers as "industry's guide to the East European market." Sample titles of recent articles: "The Importance of Soviet-American Trade," "GDR: Point of Attraction for Leading Industrialized Capitalist Countries," "US Trade with Socialist Countries." Averages 36 pages per issue. Published every two months by Symposium Press, 245 Mamaronek Avenue, White Plains, New York 10605. $50.00 per year; $25.00 for individuals associated with subscribing institutions. (M; N/M) Since 1968.

Anglo-Soviet Journal. Surveys, reports, and articles by Soviet and British authors on the arts, literature, science, and politics in the USSR. Emphasis on cultural relations between Great Britain and the Soviet Union. Short stories; poems; reports on exhibitions and tours in the USSR; book reviews; letters to the editor from Soviet and British readers. Sample titles of recent articles: "Ivan the Terrible in Ballet," "Fedor Abramov and the Reality of Kolkhoz Life," "How Marvellous Are these Fairy Tales." 30 to 50 pages per issue. Published quarterly by the Society for Cultural Relations with the USSR, 310 Brixton Road, London SW9 6AB, England. 50 pence per issue. (M; N/M) Since 1937.

Anglo-Ukrainian News (see Ukrainian Review).

Annual Bibliography of British Writings on the U.S.S.R. and Eastern Europe (see ABSEES).

Asia Letter. Focus on political and economic conditions and developments in Asia and on commercial opportunities there for Western
businessmen and women. Many reports cover nonsocialist countries in Asia; others deal with Asian socialist countries, such as
Vietnam, Laos, and the People's Republic of China. Presented
as " 'The' authoritative analysis of Asian affairs." Articles carry
no headings. Samples of relevant topics covered in recent issues:
China's sale of tin was a major factor in depressing the international tin market; Americans living in Asia and elsewhere abroad
will be able to vote in U.S. national elections; the new rulers of
Cambodia are slowly consolidating their power and the country
will follow an independent, unified, peaceful, neutral, and non-
aligned foreign policy. Four pages per issue. Published weekly
by the Asia Letter Ltd., P.O. Box 3477, Sheungwan Post Office,
Hong Kong. Obtainable from the Asia Letter Ltd., P.O. Box 54149,
Los Angeles, California 90054. $100.00 per year. (N/M) Since
1964.

Asia Quarterly (successor to the Journal of Southeast Asia and the
Far East). Interdisciplinary journal on Asia with emphasis on economics, politics, and history. Carries articles on China regularly
and on other socialist countries in Asia occasionally. Sample titles
of recent articles: "China's Industrialization and Foreign Trade,"
"Historical and Psychological Obstacles to Japan's Rapprochement
with China," "The Future of Communism in South Asia." About
75 to 85 pages per issue. Published quarterly by the Centre d'Etude
du Sud-Est Asiatique et de l'Extreme-Orient, Avenue Jeanne 44,
B-1050 Brussels, Belgium. 500 Belgium francs per year. (N/M)
Since 1971.

Asian Affairs, An American Review. Interdisciplinary journal of
Asian affairs with major emphasis on politics. Articles on U.S.
policy in Asia, on domestic policies and economics of the Asian
countries, and on their international relations. Many articles on
the socialist countries of Asia. Sample titles of recent articles
dealing with socialist countries: "China's Military-Industrial Complex: Its Influence on National Security Policy," "Vietnam After
the Cease-Fire," "Moscow's Southeast Asia Offensive." About
72 pages per issue. Published every two months by American-
Asian Educational Exchange, 88 Morningside Drive, New York,
N.Y. 10027. $12.00 per year. (N/M) Since 1973.

Asian Outlook (formerly Free China and Asia). Illustrated magazine
focusing on conditions and developments in Asia that affect the Republic of China and the People's Republic of China. A part of each
issue is devoted to the latter and to Chinese communism specifi-

cally. Declared purpose: "to provide information, analyses, and a public forum on the affairs of Asia, with the view of augmenting the strength of freedom among the Asian peoples." Sample titles of recent articles dealing with mainland China or with communism in Asia: "Kim Il Sung's Visit to Peiping," "The New Political Storm on the Chinese Mainland," "New Situation after the Fall of Indochina." 36 to 48 pages per issue. Published monthly at 1 Tsingtao East Road, Taipei, Taiwan, Republic of China. Obtainable from Asian Outlook, P.O. Box 22992, Taipei, Taiwan, Republic of China. $2.00 per year; airmail, $5.00 extra. (N/M) Since 1954.

Association for Comparative Economic Studies: Bulletin (see ACES Bulletin).

ASTE Bulletin (see ACES Bulletin).

B.B.C. Monitoring Service. Reports on foreign radio broadcasts and news agency transmissions, concentrating mainly on those areas where other sources of information are not readily accessible. More than 100 countries, with more than 50 languages, are covered—major official sources, such as Moscow radio, as well as, for example, provincial stations in the People's Republic of China.
The B.B.C. Monitoring Service offers four periodic publications in English:
    1. Summary of World Broadcasts (SWB).
Transcripts in English translation of the above material, varying from full texts of important pronouncements to brief items of factual information. Published daily, except Sundays and public holidays, in four parts. All but Part 4 include one or more of the 16 socialist countries covered in this index:
    Part 1: The USSR—22 pages per issue
    Part 2: Eastern Europe—26 pages per issue
    Part 3: The Far East (and other regions of Asia)—35 pages per
        issue
    Part 4: The Middle East and Africa—23 pages per issue
£50 per part per year, plus postage of £20 for surface mail and £70 for airmail to the United States. (Subscribers primarily interested in, for example, Soviet Broadcasts [Part 1] may additionally subscribe to those sections of other parts that cover broadcasts to or about the USSR.)
    2. Weekly Economic Report.
Supplements to each of the four parts of the SWB, containing information about agriculture and industry, trade agreements, natural

resources, and scientific and technical progress. Supplement to Part 1 (see above) is 25 pages per issue; to Part 2, 25 pages; to Part 3, 36 pages, and to Part 4, 14 pages. All supplements are published weekly. £30 per supplement per year, plus postage of £4 for surface mail and £10 for airmail to the United States.

    3. Monitoring Report.
Highlights from the SWB. Also includes points from broadcasts from Latin American and other countries not covered in the SWB. Six pages per issue. Published daily. £30 per year, plus postage of £20 for surface mail and £35 for airmail to the United States.

    4. World Broadcasting Information (WBI).
Developments in broadcasting around the world and transmission schedules and frequencies used by broadcasting organizations. Length varies. Published weekly. £15 per year, plus postage of £4 for surface mail and £10 50s for airmail to the United States.

All four periodic publications are obtainable from Organizer, News and Publications, B.B.C. Monitoring Service, Caversham Park, Reading RG4 8TZ, England. (M; N/M) Since 1959.

Booklets on Hungary. Illustrated booklets, each dealing with some aspect of life in Hungary. Sample titles of recently published books and of articles in them: Social Services in Hungary—"New Health Act," "Topics for Debate: Birth Rate Too Low," "Special Association Helps the Blind"; Young Hungary—"Youth at Work," "Youth and Law: Young Offenders," "Youth and Politics"; Hungary: Life Today—"Shops and Services," "The Farm Worker," "Churches and Church Life." 64 pages per booklet. Published intermittently by the Press Section of the Embassy of the Hungarian People's Republic, 16 Lowndes Close, London SWIX 8 BZ, England. Free (M)

Books from Hungary (see HUNGARIAN BOOK REVIEW).

Bridge. Literary review with emphasis on Yugoslav literature. Some articles in English, others in French or German. Sample titles of recent English-language articles: "Five Zagreb Literary Talks," "Macedonian Poetry Today," "Trends in Contemporary Irish Poetry." About 100 to 150 pages per issue. Published every two months by the Association of Croatian Writers, Trg Republike 7, Zagreb, Yugoslavia. $9.00 per year. (M) Since 1966.

British-Soviet Friendship. Illustrated magazine. Features articles on all aspects of life in the Soviet Union, with special emphasis on Anglo-Soviet relations. Declared purpose: "Non-party, non-sectarian, to promote peace, friendship & trade for the mutal benefit

of Great Britian & the Soviet Union." Book reviews; letters to the
editor. Sample titles of recent articles: "Milestone in Manchester-
Leningrad Relations," "The Peace Idea—And Soviet Contribution,"
"Co-ops Boost Living Standards in Soviet Countryside." 16 pages
per issue. Published every two months by the British-Soviet
Friendship Society, 36 St. John's Square, London ECIV 4JH, England. 90 pence per year, plus overseas postage; free to members
of the British-Soviet Friendship Society; membership dues: £2 per
year. (N/M) Since 1955.

BTA News Bulletin. News reports from Bulgaria. Sections on politics, economics, culture, science and technology, education, medicine and health, social welfare, archaeology, sports, and "the
week," consisting of brief, usually one-sentence, reports of news
events of the past week. Sample titles of recent articles: "Economic Integration with the USSR," "Cultural Activity of Trade Unions,"
"Stanko Todorov's Visit to the GDR." 14 pages per issue. Published weekly by the Bulgarian Telegraph (News) Agency (BTA),
49 Boulevard Lenin, Sofia, Bulgaria. $30.00 per year. (M)

Bulgaria (see Bulgaria Today).

Bulgaria Today (formerly Bulgaria). Pictorial magazine. Focus on
all aspects of life in Bulgaria. Some articles on other topics of
general interest or of special interest to Bulgarian Marxist-Leninists. Some short stories and cartoons. Letters to the editor;
questions by readers and answers by the editors. Sample titles of
recent articles: "Vocational Training in Bulgaria," "Scientific and
Technical Cooperation between Bulgaria and India," "Women as
Seen by Men." 30 pages per issue. Published monthly by the Sofia
Press Agency, 1 Levski Street, Sofia, Bulgaria. $3.00 per year.
(M) Since 1964.

Bulgarian Films. Pictorial magazine. Articles about Bulgarian mo-
tion pictures. Detailed film reviews. Brief "News Items" such as
"GDR-Cuban Film Shot in Bulgaria," or "Prize Winning Young
Bulgarian Actors." Sample titles of recent articles: "Bulgarian
Film Art at a New Stage," "Director Ivan Terziev," "The Sixth
Red Cross and Health Film Festival—Varna—1975." About 20
pages per issue. Published eight times per year by State Film
Distribution, 135 Rakovsky Street, Sofia, Bulgaria. $30.00 per
year. (M) Since 1960.

Bulgarian Foreign Trade. Pictorial magazine. Focus on aspects of
the Bulgarian economy that affect Bulgaria's international economic relations and especially its exports. Full-page ads of products

offered for sale abroad. Sample titles of recent articles: "Scientific and Technical Progress in Bulgaria," "Major Joint Development Projects," "New Products of the May Day Cannery." 48 pages per issue. Published every two months by Bulgarreklama Agency, 42 Parchevich Street, Sofia 42, Bulgaria. Free. (M) Since 1950.

Bulgarian Historical Review. Articles primarily on the economic, political, and cultural history of Bulgaria. Covers antique, medieval, modern, and contempory history. Reports on conventions of historical societies meeting in Bulgaria. Abstracts; book reviews; bibliographies. Declared purpose: "The chief aim is to throw light upon the scientific achievements of Bulgarian historians on problems pertaining to Bulgaria, the Balkans and general history." Sample titles of recent articles: "The Bulgarian National Liberation Movement at the Beginning of the 19th Century," "The Ancient Baltic Peoples," "Archaeological Investigations in Bulgaria in the Last Few Decades." Averages about 125 pages per issue. Published quarterly by the United Center for Research and Training in History at the Bulgarian Academy of Sciences, Editorial Office, Capaev Street, B. 9, Sofia 13, Bulgaria. Obtainable from VTD Hemus, Ruski 6, Sofia, Bulgaria. Eight levas per year. (M) Since 1973.

Bulgarian News and Views (formerly Bulgarian News Release; before that, News from Bulgaria). News items on all aspects of life in Bulgaria. Declared purpose: "to promote knowledge of Bulgaria, its foreign policy, industrial and social progress." Sample titles of recent articles: "The State and the Trade Union in Bulgaria," "British Firms at Plovdiv 31st Trade Fair," "The Cyprus Problem, the Balkans and Bulgaria." Averages about ten pages per issue. Prepared in collaboration with the Sofia Press Agency and published monthly by the Press Department of the Embassy of the People's Republic of Bulgaria, 12 Queen's Gate Gardens, London SW7, England. Free to newspapers, radio and television stations, journalists, and so on. (M)

Bulgarian News Release (see Bulgarian News and Views).

Bulgarian Studies Group Newsletter. Reports on relevant conferences; announcements of forthcoming conferences; listings and descriptions of research opportunities; abstracts of recent and current research carried out by scholars in the field. Declared purpose: to inform the members of the Bulgarian Studies Group (BSG) of "scholarly work in all disciplines having to do with Bulgaria," and, secondarily, to develop and maintain good relations with scholarly institutions in Bulgaria. Averages about 15 pages per

issue. Published twice a year by the Center for Russian and East
European Studies, Cocke Hall, University of Virginia, Charlottes-
ville, Virginia 22903. Distributed free to members of the BSG and
to other interested scholars. The latter, however, are urged to
become dues-paying members ($3.00 per year) of the BSG. (N/M)

Bulgarian Trade Unions. Illustrated magazine. Concentrates primar-
ily on aspects of economic, political, social, and cultural life in
Bulgaria and on topics of special interest to trade union members.
Occasional biographic sketches of outstanding Bulgarian workers.
Sample titles of recent articles: "The Labour Laws and the Status
of Bulgarian Women," "A Glimpse at Industrial Sofia," "How Can
We Best Use Our Long Week-end?" 64 pages per issue. Published
every two months by the Central Council of the Bulgarian Trade
Unions, 83 Dondoukov Boulevard, Sofia, Bulgaria. Price not given;
was $3.00 per year in 1973. (M) Since 1966.

Bulletin of the Association for Comparative Economic Studies (see
ACES Bulletin).

Bulletin of Foreign Commercial Information. Covers a wide range of
commercial and economic topics, including economic and business
conditions abroad, the work of international economic organizations,
market trends for main items in international trade, international
trade prices, and monetary policies of foreign countries. Based
on reports from the Soviet news agency Tass and from foreign news
agencies. Some 200 supplements per year, including "Contemporary Situation of the Capitalist Economies and the Conditions of the
Main Commodity Markets." Published three times a week by the
USSR Ministry of Foreign Trade, 4 Pudovkin Street, Moscow,
USSR. Obtainable from Mezhdunarodnaya Kniga, G-200, USSR.
Price not given. (M)

Bulletin of Novosti Press Agency. Illustrated newspaper. Primary
emphasis on the struggle of "national liberation" movements, of
Marxist, and of other opposition groups in nonsocialist countries.
Sample titles of recent articles: "Gestapo and the Chilean Police:
Ideological Affinity," "Freedom to Political Prisoners in the Republic of South Africa," "Nambia: Terror and Genocide." Generally four to eight pages per issue. Published irregularly by the
Novosti Press Agency, Moscow. Price varies, usually two to
three kopeks per issue. (M)

Bulletin of Soviet Jewish Affairs (see Soviet Jewish Affairs).

Bulletin: Statni Banka Ceskoslovenska (see Statni Banka Ceskoslovenska: Bulletin).

Canadian-American Review of Hungarian Studies. Interdisciplinary journal covering all fields of Hungarian studies, with emphasis on history. Book reviews and reviews of book reviews published in other periodicals. Sample titles of recent articles: "Horthy, Hitler and the Hungary of 1944," "Recent Publications in Hungarian Art History," "Hungarian Studies at American and Canadian Universities." About 70 pages per issue. Occasional supplement containing research, publishing, and relevant personal news items. Published twice a year by the Hungarian Readers Service under the editorship of Dr. N. F. Dreisziger, Department of History, Royal Military College of Canada, Kingston, Ontario, Canada K7L 2W3. Obtainable from Dr. Ferenc Harscar, 908-1356 Meadowlands Drive East, Ottawa, Ontario, Canada K2E 6K6. $12.00 per year; $20.00 for two years; $8.00 per year for students' and teachers' personal subscriptions. (N/M) Since 1974.

Canadian American Slavic Studies (formerly Canadian Slavic Studies). Interdisciplinary journal dealing with the Soviet Union and East Europe. Some emphasis on history and literature. Book reviews. Sample titles of recent articles: "The Russian Aristocracy and the Reforms of Peter the Great, Dostoevski's Notes from the Underground and Hegel's 'Master and Slave,'" "Bank Credit and the Labor-Managed Firms: The Yugoslav Case." Published quarterly by the University Center for International Studies (UCIS), University of Pittsburgh, 218 Oakland Avenue, Pittsburgh, Pennsylvania 15260, in conjunction with Temple University and with the support of the International Center for European Studies, Concordia University. Obtainable from UCIS Publications Section, University Center for International Studies, C-6 Mervis Hall, University of Pittsburgh, Pittsburgh, Pennsylvania 15260. $15.00 per year for institutions; $12.50 for faculty; $8.00 for full-time students. Lower prices for subscribers taking more than one UCIS journal. For more specific information on reduced rates, see UCIS Journals. (N/M) Since 1966.

Canadian Slavic Studies (see Canadian American Slavic Studies).

Canadian Slavonic Papers. Interdisciplinary journal in the field of Slavic and East European studies. Features articles dealing with history, government, international relations, economics, geography, literature, philosophy, linguistics, and so on, all relating to the Soviet Union and East Europe. Most articles in English with French summaries; some in French with English summaries. Book reviews. Sometimes an entire issue devoted to one topic, such as "Alexander Solzhenitsyn," "Russian and Soviet Central

Asia," "Poland in the 1970's." Sample titles of recent articles:
"Post Munich Czechoslovakia: A Few Historical Notes," "Belorus-
sia: Modernization, Human Rights, Nationalism," "Eastern European Studies in the West as Seen from Eastern Europe." Averages
about 160 pages per issue. Subscribers also receive Etudes Slaves
et Est-Européennes/Slavic and East European Studies, an interdisciplinary journal with some articles in French, others in English, and with emphasis on Slavic literature; averages 120 pages
per issue, published annually, not sold separately. Canadian Slavonic Papers is published quarterly by the Canadian Association
of Slavists, 256 Paterson Hall, Carleton University, Ottawa, Canada KlS 5B6. Free to members of the Canadian Association of
Slavists (membership dues: $15.00 per year in Canadian funds or
equivalent); $15.00 per year to nonmembers. (A cumulative index
for volumes 1 through 15 was published in 1974 and is available
for $3.00.) (M; N/M) Since 1956.

Central Europe Journal. Political, social and economic developments
in Central Europe. Many articles on West Germany, but others on
Czechoslovakia, on West German relations with socialist countries
in East Europe, and on related topics. Book reviews. Sample titles of recent articles: "Germans and Czechs: A Tragic Historical
Example," "International Organizations in East-West Relations,"
"Reciprocal Tourism with the European East." Averages about
45 pages per issue. Published every two months by the Edition
Atlantic Forum, Kurt-Schumacher Str. 1, D-53 Bonn 12, Germany.
$8.00 per year. (N/M) Since 1953.

China and US. Articles on conditions, developments, and various aspects of life in China. Announcements aimed at Americans interested in friendship with China. Poems; letters to the editor. Sample titles of recent articles: "A Green Heart: Notes on Children's
Cultural Activities in China," "China's Minority: The Tajik Story,"
"New York Friends Pay Tribute to Chou-En-Lai." 16 pages per
issue. Published every two months by the US-China Peoples Friendship Association, 41 Union Square West, Room 1228, New York,
N.Y. 10003. Free to members of the association; membership
dues: $6.00 per year, $3.00 for students, the unemployed, and
retired persons. (N/M)

China Exchange Newsletter. Reports on visitors and delegations to
and from China, on Chinese exchanges with the United States and
with other countries, on Chinese attendance at international meetings, and on related topics. Selected bibliography on China. Sample titles of recent reports: "Scholarly Exchange in 1976," "OECD

Conference on Science in China," "Scientific and Technical Association Delegation Completes U.S. Visit: Future Exchanges Discussed." Six to eight pages per issue. Published every two months by the Committee on Scholarly Communication with the People's Republic of China (CSCPRC), National Academy of Sciences, 2101 Constitution Avenue, Washington, D.C. 20418. Free. (N/M) Since 1973.

China Letter. Focus on political and economic conditions and developments in China and on commercial opportunities there for Western businessmen and women. "China Chronology" of relevant issues, such as the opening of a fair, the establishment of diplomatic relations between China and another country, or the arrival of a foreign diplomat in China. Researched and written on the scene in Hong Kong by a staff of China "watchers" and China travelers. Articles carry no headings. Samples of relevant topics covered in recent issues: changing purpose of China's twice-yearly export commodities fair; history and prospects of China's oil production; virtual abandonment of international regulations of sale of militarily sensitive equipment and materials to China. Eight pages per issue. "Special Report" two-page supplements, sometimes more than one per issue, on specific topics, such as China's increasing interest in greatly extending relations with the Philippines. Published monthly by the Asia Letter Ltd., P.O. Box 3477, Sheungwan Post Office, Hong Kong. Obtainable from the Asia Letter Ltd., P.O. Box 54149, Los Angeles, California 90054. $175.00 per year. (N/M) Since 1971.

China News Analysis. Newsletter focusing on political, economic, social, and cultural affairs, conditions, and developments in China. Occasional articles on Vietnam. Sample titles of recent articles: "Shifting Balance of Power in Peking," "Health in the Villages," "South Vietnam under the Communists." Seven pages per issue. Published weekly at P.O. Box 13225, Hong Kong. $96.00 per year; airmail, $8.00 extra. (N/M) Since 1953.

China Notes. Material on China deemed to have a religious or a human dimension. Some articles on organizations of Chinese society. Book reviews. Sample titles of recent articles: "Christian Voices from the Church in China: A Report of Recent Conversations with Christians in the People's Republic of China," "Prevention and Treatment of Mental Illness in the People's Republic of China," "China's Bourgeois Rights Campaign." 12 pages per issue. Published quarterly by the East Asia Office of the National Council of Churches, 475 Riverside Drive, Room 616, New York, N.Y. 10027. $2.00 per year. (N/M) Since 1963.

China Now. Articles sympathetic to the People's Republic of China, dealing with conditions, developments, and various aspects of life in China. Book reviews. Sample titles of recent articles: "Psychiatry in Shanghai," "China's International Policy," "Child Care in China." Published ten times per year by the Society for Anglo-Chinese Understanding, 152 Camden High Street, London NW1 ONE, England. $14.00 per year; $18.00 by airmail. (N/M) Since 1970.

China Pictorial. Pictorial magazine. Focus on conditions, developments, and various aspects of life in China and on China's international relations. Special emphasis on economic achievements and progress and on political affairs. Section on "Important Events," "A Warm Welcome to Distinguished Guests From . . ." and "Photographs from Readers." Sample titles of recent articles: "Tatchai's Children's Out of School Activities," "Heroic Road Maintenance Crew," "Tanzania Strides Forward." About 45 pages per issue. Published monthly at Chegongzhuang Road, Peking 28, China. Obtainable from Guozi Shudian, P.O. Box 399, Peking, China. $4.00 per year; $6.00 for two years: $8.00 for three years. (M) Since 1951.

China Policy Study Group Broadsheet. Focus on China's internal developments, foreign policy, and ideological orientation. Occasional book reviews. Sample titles of recent articles: "China's Revolution in Education," "A Year of People's Victories in Southeast Asia and China," "China and Albania: A Model of Proletarian Internationalism." Four pages per issue. Published monthly by the China Policy Study Group, 62 Parliament Hill, London NW3 2TJ, England. $6.00 per year open, $8.60 sealed; airmail $7.85 per year open, $11.20 sealed. (M) Since 1964.

China Quarterly. Emphasis on political, economic, social, and educational developments in China. Book reviews. Sample titles of recent articles: "Centralization and Decentralization in China's Fiscal Management," "New Light on Mao: Quemoi, 1958: Mao's Miscalculations," "Recent Developments in China's University Recruitment System." About 200 pages per issue. Published by the Contemporary China Institute of the School of Oriental and African Studies, London University, Malet Street, London WCIE 7HP, England. Obtainable from Research Publications Ltd., Victoria Hall, East Greenwich, London SE10 ORF, England. $10.00 per year; $5.00 for full-time students. (N/M) Since 1960.

China Reconstructs. Illustrated magazine. Articles and reports on politics, economics, education, public health, science, literature, art, women, history, geography, and so on in China and on China's foreign relations. Special sections on culture; sports; children's stories; stamps. Chinese language lessons. Section entitled "From the Revolutionary Past." Sample titles of recent articles: "How China Solved Her Food Problem," "Revolutionary Culture at the Cross Roads," "Women of New China." 48 pages per issue. Published monthly at Wai Wen Building, Peking (37), China. Obtainable from Guozi Shudian, P.O. Box 339, Peking, China. $3.00 per year; $4.50 for two years; $6.00 for three years. (M) Since 1952.

China Report. Empirical and theoretical studies of contemporary China in all its aspects. Some emphasis on economics and politics. Declared purpose: "To encourage in its pages a free discussion of different ideas and points of view on China . . . adequately substantiated or otherwise documented." Sample titles of recent articles: "Unemployment and Underemployment in the People's Republic of China," "Emancipation and Enslavement of Women in China: Confucian and Communist Variations," "Japan-China Peace Pact: Problems and Prospects." 60 pages per issue. Published six times a year by the Centre for the Study of Developing Societies, 29 Rajpur Road, Delhi 6, India. $10.00 per year for regular subscriptions; $12.00 for institutions; $4.00 for students. (N/M) Since 1969.

China Trade and Economic Newsletter. Trade news; interpretations of commercial and economic developments in China; extensive statistics which include a detailed break-down of British import and export trade with China, and frequent features on the composition of the China trade of other countries, recently, for instance, of Japan, Canada, Australia, and the USA. Book reviews; some pictures. Sample titles of recent articles: "Focus Shifts to Electronics," "Notes for the China Trader," "No Steel Cut-Back in China." About 10 to 12 pages per issue. Published monthly at 25 Bedford Row, London, WC1R 4HE, England. Subscription rates include stiff printed binder. $31.00 per year; $40.00 by airmail. (N/M) Since 1955-56.

China Trade Report. Focus on conditions, developments, and news items related to China's foreign trade. Some detailed surveys, for instance, on port developments, on specific industries, and on patterns of China's trade with socialist countries. Political comments relevant to trade. Trade statistics; reports on delegations to and from China. Described by the publishers as "a comprehensive monthly analysis of market trends and commercial pol-

icies of the People's Republic of China." Sample titles of recent
articles: "Price Spiral," "Peking in 2-1/2 Hours," "Malaysia's
Trade with China." 16 pages per issue. Published monthly by Far
Eastern Economic Review, Ltd., P.O. Box 160, Hong Kong. Obtainable from Circulation Manager, P.O. Box 47, Hong Kong.
$84.00 per year. (M; N/M) Since 1962.

China Trade Telegram. Published monthly by Cognizant Corporation,
P.O. Box 216, Croton-on-Hudson, New York 10520. $150.00 per
year. (U) Since 1974. (No further information procured.)

China's Foreign Trade. Pictorial magazine. Focus on events, conditions, developments, and policies directly pertinent to China's
international economic relations, and especially to the exportation
of Chinese products. Ads of products China offers for sale abroad.
Sample titles of recent articles: "Constant Economic and Technical Cooperation Development between China and Friendly Countries," "Exporting China's Textile Products," "Developing Lienyun
Harbor." About 48 to 60 pages per issue. Published quarterly by
the Council for the Promotion of International Trade, Peking, China. Obtainable from Guozi Shudian, P.O. Box 399, Peking, China.
$3.00 per year; $4.50 for two years; $6.00 for three years; air-
mail $12.00 per year. (M)

Chinese Economic Studies. Unabridged translations of articles on aspects of the Chinese economy, and sometimes on Marxist economic theory, taken from Chinese sources, primarily scholarly
journals and collections of articles in book form. Occasional contributions by Western authors. Usually each issue is devoted to a
single topic, such as Land Reform and Economic Development in
China, Fundamentals of Political Economy, Visitors' Reports on
the Chinese Economy (Western). About 100 pages per issue. Published quarterly by the International Arts and Sciences Press,
901 North Broadway, White Plains, New York 10603. $70.00 per
year for institutions; $20.00 for individuals associated with sub-
scribing institutions. (M; N/M) Since 1956.

Chinese Education. Unabridged translations of articles in the field
of Chinese education, taken from Chinese sources, primarily
scholarly journals and collections of articles in book form. Frequently either substantial parts of an issue or an entire issue devoted to a single topic, such as "Student Admissions Policies and
Procedures," "Teaching Methods for Science and Technology,"
"The Campaign Against Confucius and Confucianism." About 120
to 150 pages per issue. Published quarterly by the International
Arts and Sciences Press, 901 North Broadway, White Plains, New

York 10603. $70.00 per year for institutions; $20.00 for individuals associated with subscribing institutions. (M) Since 1968.

Chinese Law and Government. Unabridged translations of articles in the general area of law and government in China, taken from Chinese sources, primarily from scholarly journals and from collections of articles in book form. Sample titles of recent articles: "Mao Tse-tung's Sixty Articles on Work Methods," "The Fundamental Differences between the Proletarian and Bourgeois Military Lines," "Judicial Work in T'ai-hang." Published quarterly by the International Arts and Sciences Press, 901 North Broadway, White Plains, New York 10603. $70.00 per year for institutions; $20.00 for individuals associated with subscribing institutions. (M) Since 1968.

Chinese Literature. Essays, short stories, poetry, excerpts from novels, songs, art reproductions, and so on. Also articles on Chinese policies on literature and art. Announcements of literary and art events. Described by the publishers as "a literary magazine that reflects the new outlook and new life of the people of this multi-national land in the period of socialist revolution and construction." Sample titles of recent articles: "A New Revolutionary Dance Drama," "New Children's Songs from a Peking Primary School," "The Struggle Between the Confucians and the Legalists in the History of Chinese Literature and Art." About 110 to 116 pages per issue. Published monthly by the Foreign Languages Press, Peking 37, China. Obtainable from Guozi Shudian, P.O. Box 399, Peking, China. $4.00 per year; $6.00 for two years; $8.00 for three years. (M) Since 1951.

Chinese Sociology and Anthropology. Unabridged translations of articles in the fields of sociology and anthropology taken from Chinese sources, primarily scholarly journals and collections of articles in book form. One or more issues are devoted to a single topic, such as "Historical Materials on the South Sea Brothers Tobacco Factory," "Changes at the Shanghai Harbor Docks," "Why our Marital Relationship Has Broken Down." 80 to 110 pages per issue. Published quarterly by the International Arts and Sciences Press, 901 North Broadway, White Plains, New York 10603. $70.00 per year for institutions; $20.00 for individuals associated with subscribing institutions. (M) Since 1968.

Chinese Studies in History. Unabridged translations of articles in the field of Chinese history taken from Chinese sources, primarily scholarly journals and collections of articles in book form. Occasionally an entire issue is devoted to a single topic, such as

"The First Emperor of China." Sample titles of recent articles:
"A New Variation of the 'Idea that History Is Made by Heroes,' "
"The Historic Development and Aggressive Nature of American
Imperialist Investment in China (1784-1914)," "The Provincial
Leadership of the People's Republic of China after the Tenth Par-
ty Congress." Averages about 100 pages per issue. Published
quarterly by the International Arts and Sciences Press, 901 North
Broadway, White Plains, New York 10603. $70.00 per year for
institutions; $20.00 for individuals associated with subscribing
institutions. (M) Since 1967.

Chinese Studies in Philosophy. Unabridged translations of relevant
articles taken from Chinese sources, primarily scholarly journals
and collections of articles published in book form. Articles cover
a cross section of subjects discussed by Chinese Marxist philosophers today. Occasionally an entire issue is devoted to a single
topic, such as "Aesthetics in the People's Republic of China."
Sample titles of recent articles: "The Philosophical Significance of
Natural Science History Research," "My Option between Philosophy
and Religion," "On the Methodology of the History of Philosophy
and the Problem of the Inheritance of Morals: A Tentative Treatise
on the Buddhist Philosophical Thought of Hui-Yuan." About 100
pages per issue. Published quarterly by the International Arts and
Sciences Press, 901 North Broadway, White Plains, New York
10603. $70.00 per year for institutions; $20.00 for individuals
associated with subscribing institutions. (M) Since 1969.

Chronicle of Current Events. Translation of a periodical produced
underground in typewritten form in the Soviet Union and circulated
there in chain-letter fashion. Concentrates on alleged violations
of human rights in the USSR and on conditions in labor camps and
psychiatric hospitals. Occasional pictures, maps showing the main
places mentioned, glossaries, and reproductions of pages from the
original Russian-language samizdat (underground) periodical. O-
ver 150 pages per issue, subject to change. Published irregularly
by Amnesty International Publications, 200 West 72nd Street, New
York, N.Y. 10023. $2.50 per copy, plus 50 cents for postage and
handling. (N/M) Since 1968.

Chronicle of Human Rights in the USSR. Focus on alleged violations
of human rights in the USSR. Reports on arrests and trials of individuals charged with offenses such as anti-Soviet agitation. Documents. Sections on "Activities of Organizations Concerned with
Human Rights" and "Western Activities in Defense of Human Rights
in the USSR." Bibliography of relevant new books. About 64 pages

per issue. Published every two months by the Khronika Press, 505 Eighth Avenue, New York, N. Y. 10018. $20.00 per year for institutions; $15.00 for individuals; $10.00 for students and emigrants to Israel. (N/M) Since 1973.

CIA Office of Economic Research Aids. Unclassified monographs entailing documented research on a variety of economic topics, many of them dealing with economic affairs in the Soviet Union and China. Extensive use of charts, graphs, and tables. Sample topics of recent volumes: "People's Republic of China: Foreign Trade in Machinery and Equipment since 1952," "The Soviet Economy: 1974 Results and 1975 Prospects," "The Soviet Grain Balance, 1960-73." Volumes vary in length from a few to several hundreds of pages. Published irregularly (for instance, six in 1974, more than twice as many in 1975) by the Office of Economic Research of the U.S. Central Intelligence Agency, Washington, D.C. 20505. Issued primarily for the use of U.S. government officials. Obtainable by non-U.S. government users from Document Expediting (DOCEX) Project, Exchange and Gifts Division, Library of Congress, Washington, D.C. 20540. $225.00 per year. (Price quotation for electrostatic positive print or microfilm copies of individual titles available from Photoduplication Service, Library of Congress, 10 First Street, S.E., Washington, D.C. 20540.) Complimentary copies of individual titles occasionally sent to scholars in the field. (N/M)

Communist Viewpoint. Primarily theoretical, political, economic, and ideological articles presented from a Marxist-Leninist point of view. Some articles on the Communist party of Canada; at times, contributions by Soviet authors. Documents; book reviews; occasional letters to the editor. Sample titles of recent articles: "Democracy for Whom?" "Women and Capitalist Exploitation," "Peking's Foreign Policy Aims." 64 pages per issue. Published six times per year, currently under the editorship of Alfred Dewhurst, member of the Executive Committee of the Communist party of Canada, by Progress Books, 487 Adelaide Street West, Toronto, Ontario, Canada. $5.00 per year; $8.50 for two years. (M) Since 1969.

Contemporary Poland. Emphasis on current political, economic, and cultural developments in Poland. Review of the Polish press; chronicle (day-by-day current events) of the month. Portrait of the month. New books. Sample titles of recent articles: "The Problem of Food Supply and Nutrition in Poland," "The Younger Generation of People's Poland," "Poland's Import and Exhibitions

of Western Books." 28 to 30 pages per issue. Published monthly
by the Polish Interpress Agency, ul. Bagetela 12, 00-585 Warsaw,
Poland. Obtainable from Ruch, ul. Wronia 23, P.O. Box 154,
Warsaw, Poland. $3.00 per year. (M) Since 1967.

Croatia Press. Focus on alleged repressions and violations of human
rights in Yugoslavia, and especially in Croatia. Occasional pictures; book reviews; letters to the editor. Sample titles of recent
articles: "Four Croatian Youths Sentenced from Five to Ten Years
for Distributing Emigré Publications," "The International League
for the Rights of Man Condemns Repression of Human Rights in
Yugoslavia," "Freedom of the Press, Serbian Centralist Way:
Leading Croatian Journalists Ousted and Silenced." 24 to 32 pages
per issue. Published quarterly by Croatia Press, P.O. Box 1767,
Grand Central Station, New York, N.Y. 10017. $8.00 per year.
(N/M) Since 1947.

Cuba Economic News. Brief reports on various aspects of Cuba's
economic conditions, affairs, and developments. Some pictures.
Occasional presentation of statistical material. Sample titles of
recent articles: "Cuba Buys 110 Fishing Boats from Peru," "Cuba:
Lowest Infant Mortality Rate among Countries of Latin America,"
"Economic and Industrial Cooperation Agreement between Cuba
and Italy." Averages 20 to 24 pages per issue. Published monthly
by the Information Department of the Chamber of Commerce of
the Republic of Cuba, Box 270, Havana, Cuba. Free. (M) Since
1966.

Cuba Review. Illustrated magazine presenting a sympathetic view
toward socialist Cuba. Articles on various aspects of life in Cuba,
primarily from reports by eyewitness visitors to the island. Translations of speeches by Castro. Some documents. Declared purpose: "(1) Provide religious communities with an accurate description of the Cuban Revolution, (2) Promote communication between
North Americans and Cubans, (3) Counter United States and church
policies which contribute to injustice with respect to Cuba and Latin America." Each issue has a feature focus, such as "Blacks in
Cuba," "Schools in the Country Side," or "Religious Life." Sample titles of recent articles: "Adult and Higher Education: Every
Worker a Student, Every Student a Worker," "Image of the Catholic Church Improving," "New Values for a New Society." 24 to 36
pages per issue. Published quarterly by the Cuba Resource Center, P.O. Box 206, Cathedral Station, New York, N.Y. 10025.
$5.00 per year for individuals; $10.00 for institutions. (M; N/M)
Since 1971.

Cuban Studies (formerly Cuban Studies Newsletter). Classified bibliography of recent publications (books, chapters in books, pamphlets, and articles); description of new books; listing of current research completed and in progress; bibliographical essays and scholarly articles on contemporary themes—all relevant to Cuban studies. Sample titles of recent articles: "The Development and Application of Computer and Information Sciences in Cuba," "The Cuban Minority in the United States," "Authenticity and Autonomy in the Cuban Experience." Number of pages varies from about 60 to about 120 per issue. Published twice a year by the Center for Latin American Studies, University Center for International Studies (UCIS), University of Pittsburgh, 4200 Fifth Avenue, Pittsburgh, Pennsylvania 15213. $4.00 per year for individuals; $10.00 for institutions. (N/M) Since 1970.

Cuban Studies Newsletter (see Cuban Studies).

Culture and Life. Illustrated magazine. Primary emphasis on Soviet culture and on the relationship of the Soviet Union with other countries. Reports on the work of Soviet artists, writers, composers, and musicians and on new Soviet theater productions, films, and books. Occasional articles on other topics, including Soviet scientific and technological achievements, economic progress, and sports. Occasional sections on new Soviet postage stamps, fashions, and chess problems. Sample titles of recent articles: "The Moscow Institute of Culture," "French Literature in the Ukraine," "The Blossoming Garden of Soviet-Indian Friendship." About 48 pages per issue. Published monthly by the Union of Soviet Societies for Friendship and Cultural Relations with Foreign Countries, 13/15 Proyezd Sepunova, Moscow-Centre, USSR. Obtainable from Mezhdunarodnaya Kniga, Moscow G-200, USSR. $4.50 per year. (M) Since 1957.

Current Digest of the Soviet Press. Translations from the Soviet press on all aspects of Soviet domestic and foreign affairs. Emphasis on economic and political issues. Primary sources are the Soviet party daily Pravda and the Soviet central government daily Izvestia; however, items are also translated from more than 80 other Soviet newspapers and magazines, listed in the Current Digest. Items deemed of major importance, especially from Pravda and Izvestia, are translated in full; others are condensed, but the phraseology of the original is generally maintained. Some items deemed of yet lesser importance are paraphrased for brevity's sake and labeled "abstract." Declared purpose: to help meet the needs of scholars and journalists who "are peculiarly dependent

upon following the Soviet press closely for domestic developments,
documents, statistics, indications of official attitudes and policies,
and public declarations of the U.S.S.R." Headings are usually
translated literally, but the table of contents lists items by essen-
tial contents, as interpreted by the editors, rather than by exact
title. Sample titles of recent articles: "About Tons and Quality,"
"Greasing the Auto Mechanic's Palm," "The U.S.A.'s 'New Pacific Doctrine.'" 24 to 28 pages per issue. Subscribers also receive a quarterly, separately bound index to Current Digest translations. Published weekly by the American Association for the Advancement of Slavic Studies (AAASS), 190 West 19th Avenue, Room
254, Ohio State University, Columbus, Ohio 43210. Obtainable
from CDSP, 2043 Millikin Road, Columbus, Ohio 43210. Subscription rates (which include payments to a sustaining operational fund):
first subscription to institutions, organizations, or individuals,
$300.00 per year; each additional concurrent subscription for non-
academic subscribers, sent to the same address, $175.00 per
year; each additional, concurrent subscription for college libraries
or departments, sent to the same address, $60.00 per year; mi-
crofilm or microfiche, $100.00 per volume year. A reduced rate
of $30.00 per year may be granted to faculty, staff, and enrolled
students of academic institutions that maintain a sustaining subscription. Junior colleges and secondary schools are encouraged
to write to the business manager for reduced rates. (M) Since
1949.

Czech Books in Print. Published monthly by Artia, Ve Smeckach 30,
Prague, Czechoslovakia. (M) Since 1974. (No further information
procured.)

Czechoslovak Co-op News. Emphasis on activities and affairs of
Czechoslovak cooperatives. Primarily short, one- to three-para-
graph articles. Sample titles of recent articles· "New Statute in
the Producer Co-operatives," "Co-operative Enterprises in the
Service of Tourism," "Central Co-operative Council Scholarships."
Usually six pages per issue (except for July-August issue, which
has eight pages). Published monthly (except for a combined July-
August issue) by the Central Co-operative Council, Tesnov 5,
Prague 1, Czechoslovakia. Free. (M)

Czechoslovak Cooperator. Illustrated magazine. Covers all aspects
of life in Czechoslovakia. Primary emphasis on economic affairs,
and particularly on the cooperative movement. "Letter Box" section on international contacts ("Pen Friends Wanted"). Sample
titles of recent articles: "Present Tasks of the Central Cooperative

Council," "How People Live in Southern Bohemia," "The Federative Solution of the National Question in the CSSR." 24 pages per issue. Editorial offices: Sokolovska 140, Prague 8, Czechoslovakia. Published quarterly by, and obtainable from, the Central Co-operative Council, Tesnov 5, Prague 1, Czechoslovakia. Free (M) Since 1970.

Czechoslovak Digest. Translations, mostly from the Czechoslovak press, on politics, economics, trade, sciences, education, culture, and sports in Czechoslovakia. Includes chronology of important domestic events. Sample titles of recent articles: "Czechoslovak Cooperation with the DRV [Democratic Republic of Vietnam]," "Busy Week for Czechoslovak Delegates at UNO," "Danube—The Transcontinental Waterway." About 25 pages per issue. Published weekly by the Czechoslovak News Agency CETEKA, Opletalova 5, 11144 Prague, Czechoslovakia. $23.00 per year. (M)

Czechoslovak Economic Digest (replaces New Trends in Czechoslovak Economics). Essays, analyses, commentaries, and documents dealing with the Czechoslovak economy. Sample titles of recent articles: "Topical Questions of the Party's Economic Policy," "Thirty Years of Czechoslovak Foreign Trade," "The Share of Czechoslovak Science and Technology in the Development of Socialist Integration." About 80 pages per issue. Published eight times per year by Pragopress, Slavickova 5, 160 43, Prague, Czechoslovakia. Obtainable from Czechoslovak News Agency, Hastalska 14, 115 21 Prague 1, Czechoslovakia. $20.00 per year. (M) Since 1966.

Czechoslovak Film. Illustrated film magazine. Published quarterly by the Czechoslovak State Motion Picture Export Enterprise, Vaclaske Namesti 28, Prague 1, Czechoslovakia. Price not given; was $3.50 per year in 1970. (M) Since 1965. (No further information procured.)

Czechoslovak Film News (formerly Czechoslovak Film Press News). Published monthly by the Czechoslovak State Motion Picture Export Enterprise, Vaclaske Namesti 28, Prague 1, Czechoslovakia. Price not given. (M) Since 1965. (No further information procured.)

Czechoslovak Film Press News (see Czechoslovak Film News).

Czechoslovak Foreign Trade. Illustrated magazine. Focus on Czechoslovakia's industries, foreign trade, foreign trade policies, and foreign trade agreements. Information on activities of the Chamber of Commerce of Czechoslovakia. Announcements of trade fairs and exhibitions. Sample titles of recent articles: "The Role of the General Engineering Industry in Czechoslovakia's Economic Development," "Contractual Regulation of Economic Relations between Czechoslovakia and the Federal Republic of Germany," "Technical Services in Czechoslovak Exports to the West." About 48 pages per issue. Published monthly by the Chamber of Commerce of Czechoslovakia, Prague, Czechoslovakia. Obtainable from Rapid, ul. 28, Rijna 13, 112 79 Prague 1, Czechoslovakia. $14.00 per year. (M) Since 1961.

Czechoslovak Life. Pictorial magazine. Articles on all aspects of life in Czechoslovakia. Each issue carries a four-page pictorial spread and text on one town in Czechoslovakia, entitled "Life in Our Town." Short stories. Sample titles of recent articles: "Motor Camps in Czechoslovakia," "Czechoslovakia and the United Nations," "Pilot Scheme Paves Way for Nationwide Cancer Detection Campaign." 32 pages per issue. Published monthly by Orbis, Vinohradska 45, Prague 2, Czechoslovakia. Obtainable from Aria, Ve Smeckach 30, Prague, Czechoslovakia. $3.60 per year. (M) Since 1946.

Czechoslovak Sport. Illustrated sports review of the Czechoslovak Olympic Committee. Published quarterly at Sokolovska 140, Prague 8-Karlin, Czechoslovakia. Price not given; was 80 cents per year in 1970. (M) Since 1952. (No further information procured.)

Czechoslovak Trade Unions. Illustrated magazine. Primary emphasis on youths, workers, and trade union members—their activities and their economic and social situation. Sample titles of recent articles: "Social Security in the Czechoslovak Socialist Republic," "Holidays and Recreation—Trade Union Style," "Leisure Time and the Young Generation." 24 pages per issue. Published every two months by Czechoslovakia's Central Trade Union Council, Vaclavske Namesti 17, 112 58 Prague, Czechoslovakia. Price not given; was $2.50 per year in 1970, when it was a monthly. (M)

Czechoslovak Woman. Illustrated magazine. Published quarterly by the Czechoslovak Women's Committee, Panska 7, Box 60, Prague 1, Czechoslovakia. $2.00 per year. (M) Since 1953. (No further information procured.)

Daily News/Neueste Nachrichten. General-interest type newspaper covering Hungarian and international news items. Half in English, half in German. Published daily, except Mondays, by the Hungarian

Press Agency MTI, Budapest, Hungary. Obtainable from Kultura, P.O. Box 149, H-1389 Budapest, Hungary. $48.00 per year. (M)

Daily News Release (Hsinhua News Agency). News items from around the world, issued by the Hsinhua (New China) News Agency. Typical regional subdivision of articles: "China (domestic)," "China (foreign)," "Indochina and S.E. Asia," "Japan," "Asia and Oceania," "Arab and Africa," "Latin America," "U.S.S.R. and East Europe," "U.S.A. and West Europe," and "U.N. and International Affairs." Sample titles of recent articles: "Swift Development of Peking's Public Transport System," "Senegalese President Calls for Solidarity of Angolan Liberation Movements," "General Debate on Rhodesian Question Concludes at Fourth Committee of U.N. General Assembly." About 20 pages per issue. Published daily by China News Service, Kandachuo Building, 20, 3-chrome, Kanda, Nishiki-cho, Chiyoda-ku, Tokyo 101, Japan. $100.00 per year. (M)

Daily Report (Foreign Broadcast Information Service). Extensive coverage of news accounts, commentaries, government statements, and so on from foreign broadcasts, press agency transmissions, and newspapers and periodicals published in the respective areas and countries in the preceding 48 to 72 hours. Major emphasis on political and economic affairs, both national and international. Comes in the form of eight separate area "Daily Reports" (which include occasional supplements on particularly long speeches, party congresses, and so on):

1. People's Republic of China. Major releases of the New China News Agency and Peking Radio. Items from People's Daily (Jen-Min Jih-Pao) and Red Flag (Hung Chi.) Averages 60 pages per issue.
2. Middle East and North Africa. No socialist countries or news releases from socialist countries included. Averages 58 pages per issue.
3. Soviet Union. Texts of speeches and commentaries from Moscow Radio and Tass News Agency. Articles and editorials from major central and regional newspapers and journals, such as Pravda, Izvestia, and Krasnaya Zvezda. Averages 72 pages per issue.
4. Asia and Pacific. Radio and press coverage of nations along the western Pacific littoral (except the People's Republic of China). Press coverage includes Hanoi's Nhan Dan and Hok Tap. Averages 68 pages per issue.

5. East Europe. Speeches and commentaries from broadcasts and press agencies of Albania, Bulgaria, Czechoslovakia, the German Democratic Republic, Hungary, Poland,
Romania, and Yugoslavia. Articles and editorials from
the official press and periodicals, such as Yugoslavia's
Komunist, East Germany's Neues Deutschland, and Czechoslovakia's Rude Pravo. Averages 52 pages per issue.
6. Latin America. News reports, speeches, and commentaries from major capitals, including Havana. Press
coverage includes articles and editorials from Havana's
Granma. Averages 50 pages per issue.
7. Western Europe. Press coverage includes such Communist papers as Italy's l'Unità and France's l'Humanité.
Averages 52 pages per issue.
8. Sub-Saharan Africa. No socialist countries or news
releases from socialist countries included. Averages 22
pages per issue.

Published daily by the Foreign Broadcast Information Service,
P.O. Box 2604, Washington, D.C. 20013. Obtainable from U.S.
Department of Commerce, National Technical Information Service
(NTIS), 5285 Port Royal Road, Springfield, Virginia 22161, in the
form of paper copy reports or microfiche reports at the following
prices: paper copy reports, mailed daily: $125.00 per year for
one area report; microfiche reports, mailed weekly: $100.00 per
year for one area report; yearly rates for multiple subscription
discounts:

Number of Subscriptions	Paper Copy	Microfiche
2	$195	$160
3	265	220
4	335	280
5	405	340
6	475	400
7	545	460
8	575	500

Daily Review. Translations from the Soviet press. Includes texts of
official Soviet documents; articles on economics, industry, agriculture, foreign affairs, the Communist and working-class movement, science, art, medicine, sports, and other topics; a cross

section of current Soviet press opinion; and items of special interest from national and provincial papers. Comes in two parts.
Part One of each issue is preceded by an average of two pages of
brief summaries of news items. About three supplements per
week on "News from the Soviet Union" (short news items) or on a
specific topic, such as "Theoretical Foundations of the Leninist
Policy of Peace (Paper Presented at the Special Session of the
USSR Academy of Sciences on the Occasion of its 250th Anniversary)." Sample titles of recent articles: "USSR-Italy: Prospects
for Cooperation," "Trade Unions and Democracy," "Maoists: Ac-
complices of Colonialists." Each of the two parts averages 15
pages; "News" supplements average 8; others, 15 pages. Published daily, except Saturdays, Sundays, and national holidays, by
Novosti Press Agency, Moscow, USSR. Subscriptions accepted by
Four Continents Book Corporation, 156 Fifth Avenue, New York,
N.Y. 10010. $244.00 per year. (M)

Democratic Journalist. Articles on ideology, the history of socialist
countries, current events. Prize-winning and exceptional photos,
mainly of social conditions and of events considered of historical
significance. Published monthly by the International Organization
of Journalists, Parizka 9-11, 11001 Prague 1, Czechoslovakia.
$4.00 per year. (M) Since 1951.

Democratic People's Republic of Korea. Pictorial magazine. Covers
all aspects of life in North Korea, with special emphasis on economics, politics, and culture. Frequent critical articles on life
in South Korea. Sample titles of recent articles: "Higher Education at a [North Korean] Factory," "The National Acrobatic Art
Festival," "Miserable Plight of Children of South Korea under
U.S. Imperialist Occupation." About 33 pages per issue. Published
monthly by the Foreign Languages Publishing House, Pyongyang,
Democratic Republic of Korea. (Price not given.) (M)

Demographic Yearbook. Detailed demographic data on all vital topics,
such as births, deaths, population growth, marriage and divorce,
and migration. Tables generally broken down into continents and
further subdivided by country. Coverage includes the socialist
countries. Text in English and French. Averages about 800 pages
per issue. Published annually by the United Nations. Obtainable
from United Nations Publications, LX 2300, New York, N.Y.
10017. Price varies; the 1974 issue, for example, was $34.00 in
paperback and $42.00 clothbound. (M; N/M)

Dialectics and Humanism. Polish philosophy journal. Some emphasis
on Marxist philosophy and on Polish philosophers. Sample titles

of recent articles: "The Formation of Friedrich Engels' Weltan-
schauung," "August Cieszkowski's Philosophical Works of 1838-
1842 within the Intellectual Context of Their Times," "The Unity
and Plurality of Being According to St. Thomas." About 200 pages
per issue. Published quarterly by the Committee for Philosophical
Sciences, Institute of Philosophy and Sociology, Polish Academy
of Sciences, Warsaw, Poland. Address correspondence to Studia
Filozoficzne (for Dialectics and Humanism), Nowy Swiat 49, 00-
042 Warsaw, Poland. Obtainable from Libreria Commissionaria
Sansoni LICOSA, 45 via Lamarmora, P.O. Box 552, 50121 Flor-
ence, Italy. $10.00 per year. (M) Since 1974.

Digest of the Soviet Ukrainian Press. Translations of articles, either
in full or excerpted, from newspapers, magazines, and journals
published in the Ukraine, most of them in Kiev. Covers news items
on politics, economics, history, education, literature, Communist
party affairs, and so on in the USSR, with primary emphasis on
the Ukraine. About one page of "Brief Notes," consisting of summaries of items deemed of lesser importance by the publisher.
Sample titles of recent articles: "Kiev City Komsomol Awarded
Order of Red Banner," "Critic Demands Strict Adherence to Principles of Socialist Realism," "Economist Proposes Merging Production Associations into Large Complexes." About 30 pages per
issue. Published monthly by SUCHASNIST, Karlsplatz 8/III, 8
Munich 2, Germany. $25.00 per year; $45.00 for two years;
$60.00 for three years. Special rates for full-time students. (M)
Since 1957.

Directory of Trade. Statistical tables showing, in millions of U.S.
dollars, each country's trade with every other country for the preceding two years. Coverage includes all socialist countries. Averages about 85 to 125 pages per issue. Subscribers also receive
an Annual Supplement covering the past five years averaging over
300 pages per issue. Published monthly by the International Monetary Fund and the International Bank for Reconstruction and Development (World Bank). Obtainable from International Monetary
Fund, Washington, D.C. 20431. $10.00 per year; $3.00 for university libraries, faculty members, and students. (N/M)

Documents (see Studies and Documents).

East Asian Review. Focus on political, economic, and social affairs
and developments and on international relations of Korea, both
North and South. Declared purpose: "To meet the rising concern
about Korean Affairs, especially focused on East Asian Communist block [sic]." Sample titles of recent articles: "North Korean

Military Policy toward South Korea," "Political Socialization Process of North Korean Youth," "Polarity in East Asia and South Korea's National Security." Averages about 120 pages per issue. Published quarterly by the Institute for East Asian Studies, 130, 3-ga Chong-ro, Chongro-ku, P.O. Box 6856, Seoul, Republic of Korea. $7.00 per year. Will entertain requests for free subscriptions, normally on an exchange basis. (N/M)

East Central Europe. Interdisciplinary journal concerned with history and social science topics specifically relating to Czechoslovakia, the German Democratic Republic, Hungary, and Poland. Occasional translations and documents. Book reviews; professional news. Sample titles of recent articles: "National Historical Bibliographies in East Central Europe," "Recent Changes in Structure and Functions of the Polish Seym," "Tactics and National Unity in Prussian Poland: The Necessary Disunities." About 100 to 125 pages per issue. Published twice a year (quarterly publication planned for the future) by the University Center for International Studies (UCIS), University of Pittsburgh, 218 Oakland Avenue, Pittsburgh, Pennsylvania 15260. Obtainable from UCIS Publications Section, University Center for International Studies, C-6 Mervis Hall, University of Pittsburgh, Pittsburgh, Pennsylvania, 15260. $15.00 per year for institutions; $12.50 for faculty; $8.00 for full-time students. Lower prices to subscribers taking more than one UCIS journal. For more specific information on reduced rates, see UCIS Journals. (N/M) Since 1974.

East Europe. Emphasis on economic, political, social, and cultural affairs; conditions and developments in the Soviet Union and East Europe; and related topics. Some articles on recent history. Book reviews. Sample titles of recent articles: "The Karelians: Victims of Soviet Imperialism," "Rhodesia, Yugoslavia and the Old Double Standard," "The Molotov-Ribbentrop Pact." 31 pages per issue. Published monthly by East Europe Publishing Company, 10 East 23rd Street, New York, N.Y. 10010. $15.00 per year; $27.00 for two years. (N/M) Since 1952.

East European Quarterly. Interdisciplinary journal. Primary emphasis on history and on economic and political conditions and developments in East Europe. Most articles by scholars in the West; occasional contributions by Marxist scholars from the Soviet Union or East Europe. Book reviews. Sample titles of recent articles: "Education and Emigration as Factors in Rural Societal Development: The Russian and Polish Peasantries' Respones to Collectivization," "Yugoslav Constitutional Developments: An Expres-

sion of Growing Nationality Rights and Powers," "Eastern Europe
in the Year 2000: The Case of Poland." About 120 to 130 pages
per issue. Published quarterly by the University of Colorado, 1200
University Avenue, Boulder, Colorado 80302. $12.00 per year for
institutions; $10.00 for faculty and research scholars; $8.00 for
students. (M; N/M) Since 1967.

East European Trade. Articles, commentaries and news items focusing on the economic development of East European countries
and on their trade and economic relations with India and, secondarily, with other developing countries. Book reviews, letters to
the editor, advertisements, some pictures. 56 to 144 pages per
issue. Published monthly at A-148 Defence Colony, P.O. Box
3567, New Delhi 110024, India. $10.00 per year; $25.00 for three
years. (N/M) Since 1963.

East/West. Chinese-American newspaper presenting reports, feature articles, and analyses, primarily of life in mainland China
and of events that affect the life of Chinese in the United States.
Editors declare that views expressed are "those of the Chinese-
American and neither pro-Communist nor Nationalist China."
Some pictures; occasional poetry and letters to the editor. Advertisements, especially of establishments in San Francisco's China-
town. Sample titles of recent articles: "Bilingualism in China,"
"China Buys Aluminum from Several U.S. Firms," "Record-Break-
ing Enrollment at New York Chinese School." 16 to 20 pages per
issue. Published weekly, half in English and half in Chinese, at
758 Commercial Street, San Francisco, California 94108. $10.00
per year. (N/M) Since 1967.

East-West (Foreign Trade Board Report). Report transmitted to the
president and the Congress of the United States. Focus on commercial relations between the United States and the socialist countries. Sections on "Trade Relations," "Trade Promotion," and
"Trade Trends," followed by "Conclusions and Recommendations."
Two-thirds of the report consists of appendixes in the form of statistical tables, dealing with U.S. trade with the socialist countries
as a whole and with individual socialist countries. Published quarterly by the East-West Foreign Trade Board, U.S. Department of
the Treasury, Office of the Assistant Secretary (Trade, Energy
and Financial Resources Policy Coordination), Washington, D.C.
20220. About 50 pages per issue. Free on request. (N/M)

East-West Commerce. Focus on trade between the socialist countries
and the rest of the world. Published monthly by Foreign Corre-

spondents Ltd., 58 Paddington Street, London W1, England.
$16.00 per year. (U) Since 1954. (No further information pro-
cured.)

East-West Digest. Focus on alleged violations of human freedoms
and rights in socialist countries and Communist threats to Britain's national security. Book reviews; occasional letters to the
editor. Sample titles of recent articles: "Shelepin and Soviet Concentration Camps: The Slave Drivers and Their Sycophants, "
"Computers for the Soviets: Where Businessmen Are More Dan-
gerous than Party Members, " "Will Britain Stand Up to a Soviet
Ultimatum?" 40 pages per issue. Published every two weeks by
the Foreign Affairs Publishing Company, Ltd., 139 Petersham
Road, Richmond, Surrey, England. $12.00 per year; $24.00 by
airmail. (N/M) Since 1965.

East-West Fortnightly Bulletin. Focus on economic trends in socialist countries, on East-West trade, on internal political developments that affect socialist countries' external relations, and on
related topics. Primary emphasis on the Comecon countries (Council for Mutual Economic Assistance: Bulgaria, Cuba, Czechoslovakia, German Democratic Republic, Hungary, Mongolia, Poland,
Romania, USSR) and on Yugoslavia. Announcements of international conferences, trade fairs, exhibitions, and so on. Occasional book reviews. Sample titles of recent articles: "Hungary Re-
vises Economic Policy Tools, " "Loans for Yugoslav Steel Plant, "
"Reliability of East European Statistics. " 9 to 12 pages per issue.
Published every two weeks by East-West S.P.R.L., 13 rue Hobbema, 1040 Brussels, Belgium. 6,000 BF (Belgian francs) per
year; 6,500 BF by airmail; 11,000 BF and 12,000 BF, respectively, for two-year subscriptions. (N/M)

East-West Markets. Survey of U.S. business developments with the
Soviet Union and East Europe. Each issue is subdivided into "Pol-
icy, " "New Business, " "Finance, " "Industry, " "Technology, "
"Marketing, " "Personality, " and occasionally other sections.
Sample titles of recent articles: "Soviet Union: 1976 Grain Pro-
jection, " "GDR: Price Reforms, " "Yugoslavia: Dow Deal Near. "
Averages 12 to 16 pages per issue. Subscribers also receive an-
nual index. Published every two weeks at 1 World Trade Center,
Suite 4627, New York, N.Y. 10048. $375.00 per year. (N/M)
Since 1973.

East-West Monthly Confidential Report. Focus on economic developments in the Comecon countries (Council for Mutual Economic Assistance: Bulgaria, Cuba, Czechoslovakia, German Democratic

Republic, Hungary, Mongolia, Poland, Romania, USSR) and in
Yugoslavia, with special emphasis on investment and production
plans, new technological processes, research programs, economic legislation, and changes in management. The publishers declare that the Report "is distributed on a confidential basis, for
the eyes of the recipient only." Sample titles of recent articles:
"Soviet Coal Mining Equipment Imports," "Investment in Comecon:
A Long-Term Analysis," "Notes on Czechoslovak Chemical Fi-
bres Production." 9 to 12 pages per issue. Published monthly by
East-West S.P.R.L., 13 rue Hobbema, 1040 Brussels, Belgium.
4,000 BF (Belgian francs) per year; 4,500 BF by airmail; 7,500
BF and 8,500 BF, respectively, for two-year subscriptions.
(N/M) Since 1973.

East-West Research Reports. Monographs on the Soviet Union and
East Europe on economic topics of interest to those concerned
with East-West trade. Prepared about equally by Marxists and
non-Marxists. Sample titles of recent volumes: "Prospects for
Joint Ventures in East Europe," "Dependence of the Soviet Investment Programme on Imports of Machinery and Equipment," "Comecon Statistical Survey." About 100 to 150 pages per issue. Published irregularly, several per year, by East-West S.P.R.L., 13
rue Hobbema, 1040 Brussels, Belgium. Prices vary, recent volumes having been priced from 1,500 BF (Belgian francs) to 5,000
BF per volume. (M; N/M)

East-West Trade: World Markets. Newsletter on business and economic affairs, with emphasis on trade with Eastern Europe and
the Soviet Union. Multiple page section on "East-West Trade Report" consists of brief business news items on the USSR and on
each of the socialist countries of East Europe, except Albania.
Sample titles of recent articles: "USSR 1975 Trade Deficit," "Romania: Economic Goals Provide Opportunities for U.S. Sales,"
"RCA Contract with Poland." 16 pages per issue. Published
monthly by Robin International, Inc., 410 Park Avenue, New York,
N.Y. 10022. Obtainable from Economic News and Research, Inc.,
410 Park Avenue, 14th Floor, New York, N.Y. 10022. $65.00
per year. (N/M) Since 1964.

Eastern European Economics. Unabridged translations of articles on
economic theory, practice, and policy taken from economic journals originally published in Albania, Bulgaria, Czechoslovakia,
the German Democratic Republic, Hungary, Poland, Romania, and
Yugoslavia. Sample titles of recent articles: "The Role of Enterprise Factor Costs in the Hungarian Price System," "An Analysis

of the Effects of Yugoslav Fiscal Policy in the Light of Some New-
er Theoretical Concepts, " "The Relationship between the Economic System and Socioeconomic Development." 90 to 110 pages per
issue. Published quarterly by the International Arts and Science
Press, 901 North Broadway, White Plains, New York 10603.
$70.00 per year for institutions; $20.00 for individuals associated
with subscribing institutions. (M) Since 1962.

Eastern Horizon. Articles on all aspects of life in China and on China's historical background written by Westerners as well as by
Asians, including Chinese. Section entitled "On Many Horizons:
News and Views" dealing with news items about various countries
in Asia, including the socialist countries of Vietnam, Cambodia,
and Laos. Book reviews; pictures. Sample titles of recently published articles: "Youths in China and Their Education," "In a Peking Street," "Early European Notions of China." 68 to 72 pages
per issue. Published every two months by Eastern Horizon Press,
472 Hennessy Road, 3rd floor, Hong Kong. $4.00 per year; $7.00
for two years; $10.00 for three years. (M; N/M) Since 1960.

Echo (see Economic Echo from Yugoslavia).

Economic Bulletin for Europe. Current economic information and
statistical data, with primary emphasis on trade. Supplements
Economic Survey of Europe. Includes the Soviet Union and all the
socialist countries of East Europe, except Albania. Yugoslavia is
listed among Western European countries. Sample titles of recent articles or sections: "Trade Developments in Eastern Europe
and the Soviet Union," "East-West Trade," "A Review of East-
West Commercial Policy Developments, 1968-1973." Published
twice a year. Prepared by the Secretariat of the Economic Commission for Europe, Geneva, Switzerland. Obtainable from United
Nations Publications, LX 2300, New York, N.Y. 10017. Price
varies; in recent years, from $3.00 to $5.00 per issue. (M; N/M)
Since 1949.

Economic Echo from Yugoslavia. Pictorial magazine. Focus on con-
ditions and developments affecting Yugoslavia's international trade
and especially Yugoslavia's exports. Advertisements of goods
Yugoslavia offers for sale abroad. Sample titles of recent articles:
"The Recession in the West Has Diminished Our Export of Ready-
Made Clothes," "How to Reduce the Trade Deficit with France,"
"Increased Production Capacities of Macedonia's Textile Industry,"
About 40 to 55 pages per issue. Published quarterly at Miklosiceva
38/11, P.O. Box 271/V, 6100 Ljubljana, Slovenia, Yugoslavia.
$3.00 per issue. (M) Since 1966.

Economic News of Bulgaria. Illustrated periodical in newspaper format. Focus on economic conditions and developments in Bulgaria.
   Special emphasis on Bulgaria's economic relations with other countries. Some advertisements of products Bulgaria offers for sale
   abroad. Sample titles of recent articles: "Bulgaria-Austria: Growing Economic Relations, " "Bulgaria-USSR: Common Programme, "
   "Bulgarian Automobile Manufacture. " Six pages per issue. Published monthly by the Bulgarian Chamber of Commerce, 11a A.
   Stambolisky Boulevard, Sofia, Bulgaria. Free. (M) Since 1959.

Economic Reporter: English Supplement. Illustrated magazine. Primary emphasis on China's economy, economic system, and current economic plans and achievements. Sample titles of recent articles: "The Basic Principle of China's Foreign Trade, " "New
   China's Economic Development in 25 Years, " "China Records
   Sharp Rise in Farm Machinery Production. " 44 to 72 pages per
   issue. Published quarterly by Economic Information & Agency,
   342 Hennessy Road, 11th floor, Hong Kong. HD $3.00 (Hong Kong
   dollars) per issue. (M) Since 1966.

Economic Review. Newspaper-format periodical with primary emphasis on economic, commercial, and business news of special
   interest to Western investors in Yugoslavia. Sample titles of recent articles: "Tax on Imports of Raw Materials and Semi-finished
   Products, " "Identity of Interests—Joint Undertakings, " "Great-
   er Exports Diminish Imbalance. " Eight pages per issue. Published
   monthly at Birjuzova br. 3, Belgrade, Yugoslavia. $24.00 per
   year. (M) Since 1973.

Economic Survey of Europe (see also Economic Bulletin for Europe).
   Emphasis on recent economic developments. Detailed statistical
   information and data on output, employment, economic growth,
   prices, income, trade, and so on. Covers the Soviet Union and
   all the socialist countries of East Europe, except Albania. Yugoslavia is listed among the Western European countries. Averages
   about 150 pages per issue. Published yearly by the Secretariat of
   the Economic Commission for Europe, Geneva, Switzerland. Obtainable from United Nations Publications LX 2300, New York,
   N.Y. 10017. Price varies; in recent years, from $5.00 to $8.00
   per issue. (M; N/M)

Economics of Planning (formerly Ost-Okonomi). Articles on the theory and practice of central planning; discussion of the need for
   such planning and problems connected with it, in both socialist
   and nonsocialist countries. Book reviews. Contributions by Marxist and non-Marxist authors. Published three times per year by

the Norwegian Institute of International Affairs, Bygdoey Alle 3, Oslo 2, Norway. $11.00 per year. (M; N/M) Since 1961.

Ecotass. Soviet economic and commercial news bulletin. Regular sections on "Soviet Economy," "External Economic Relations," "Contracts," "Exhibitions," and "Statistical Section." Occasional section on "Economic and Trade Cooperation." Sample titles of recent articles: "Engineering in 1976-1980," "Coastal Trade with Japan," "Prospects of Soviet-Finnish Co-operation in the Dairy Industry." About 20 to 24 pages per issue. Published three times per week. Responsible for contents: Tass News Agency of the USSR. Obtainable from INDREBA GmbH, Aeussere Baselstrasse 297, CH-4125 Riehen, Basel, Switzerland. SWF 450 (Swiss francs) per year. (M) Since 1964.

Elta Bulletin. Reports and commentaries on Soviet affairs, with special emphasis on Lithuania and, secondarily, the Baltic region in general. Emphasis on arrests, trials, alleged violations of civil rights, and so on. Some translations from samizdat (underground) materials published in the Soviet Union. Some documents. Bibliography of relevant books, pamphlets, and articles. Sample titles of recent articles: "The Fate of the Condemned Virgilijus Jaugelis," "Baltic Nations Not Bound by Agreements Made by Others," "Medics Urged to Utilize Sickness for Atheistic Proselytism." 14 to 18 pages per issue. Published monthly by the ELTA Information Service of the Supreme Committee for Liberation of Lithuania, 29 West 57th Street, New York, N.Y. 10019. $10.00 per year. (N/M) Since 1945.

Estonian Events (see Baltic Events).

Export Administration Report. Detailed report on U.S. trade and controls over trade with the socialist countries, submitted by the secretary of commerce to the president of the United States, the president of the U.S. Senate, and the speaker of the U.S. House of Representatives. Chapters on the administration of export controls, security controls, enforcement activities, and so on for individual products or groups of products and for individual countries. Statistical data on U.S. trade with each of the socialist countries (but little information available on North Korea, North Vietnam, and Cuba; and Yugoslavia is not included, since the U.S. Department of Commerce treats Yugoslavia as a "Western" country). Over 100 pages per issue. Published twice a year (quarterly until the first quarter of 1975) by the Domestic and International Business Administration, Bureau of East-West Trade, U.S. Department of Commerce, Washington, D.C. 20230. Free. (N/M)

Export Journal. Illustrated periodical in newspaper format. Articles
on Yugoslav industry, mining, agriculture, finance, films, tourism, hunting, trade agreements, export-import, activities of business organizations, and related subjects. Emphasis on topics of
interest to exporters and importers. Advertisements, many full-
page, of Yugoslav enterprises interested in promoting the exportation of their products. Sample titles of recent articles: "Increased
Production of TV Sets, Air-Conditioning Units and Radio Receiv-
ers," "Yugoslavia in West Africa: Ready to Make Deals," "Interest in Joint Business Ventures on the Increase." 12 to 14 pages
per issue. Published twice a month by NIP Export-Press Newspaper & Publishing Enterprise, Francusca 27, 11000 Belgrade,
Yugoslavia. $15.00 per year. (M) Since 1970.

Far East Reporter. Booklets, primarily on China, showing a sympa-
thetic understanding of socialist countries in Asia. Each booklet
devoted to a specific topic. Sample titles of recent booklets:
"Building a Socialist Educational System in China," "The Past in
China's Present," "The Making of the New Human Being." Pub-
lished irregularly, usually four to five per year. Obtainable from
P.O. Box 1536, New York, N.Y. 10017. $3.00 per year. (N/M)
Since 1952.

Far Eastern Affairs. Articles on areas and countries of the Far East,
especially the socialist countries. Primary emphasis on political,
economic, and social conditions and development and on Soviet relations with countries in the Far East—all analyzed from a Soviet
point of view. Occasional articles on ideology. Sample titles of
recent articles: "China's Foreign Trade," "Maoism in the Service
of Bourgeois Ideology," "Soviet-Korean Relations: Thirty Years."
About 135 pages per issue. Published quarterly under the auspices
of the USSR Academy of Sciences, ul. Krzhizhanovskogo, dom 14,
Korp. 2 Moscow 117218, USSR. $6.00 per year. (M)

Far Eastern Economic Review. Illustrated periodical on Asian affairs. Section on "Regional Affairs" concentrates on political issues; section on "Business Affairs" on economic issues and especially on industry, finance, trade, and transportation. Some articles deal with Asia in general; some with nonsocialist, others
with socialist, countries in Asia. Monthly insert entitled Far
Eastern Economic Review FOCUS, varying in length from 20 to
over 65 pages, each devoted to some specific topic, such as "Tourism in Asia, '75," "Banking in Asia," "United States and Asia,
'75." Letters to the editor; digest of week's events in Asia; book
reviews. Sample titles of recent articles dealing with socialist

countries: "Trade: China's Stand with Japan," "Laos: When the
Rightists Become Leftists." "North Korea: Venturing into the
World." About 50 to 75 pages per issue (not counting the FOCUS
inserts). Published weekly by Far Eastern Economic Review,
Ltd., 406-410 Marina House, P.O. Box 160, Hong Kong. $26.00
per year. (N/M) Since 1946.

Far Eastern Economic Review Yearbook. Illustrated periodical (both
pictures and cartoon-type drawings) covering Australia, New Zealand, and the Far-Eastern parts of Asia. First section deals with
the region as a whole and is subdivided topically into such subsec-
tions as "Finance," "Trade and Aid," and "Population." There is
also a "News Roundup" consisting of a day-by-day report of major
political news items, covering the year. The rest of the book consists of country-by-country reviews, and it treats individually the
socialist countries of Cambodia, China, Laos, Mongolia, North
Korea, and Vietnam (in the 1975 edition, the two halves of the
country were still covered separately). The material on each country is further subdivided into "Politics," "Social Affairs," "Foreign Relations," "Economy," and "Infrastructure." Under each
country there are also several panels with important statistical
information, such as population, land area, number of schools
and hospitals, gross national product, railroad mileage, value of
exports and imports, and currency exchange rate. Over 300 pages
per issue. Published yearly by Far Eastern Economic Review,
Ltd, 406-409 Marina House, P.O. Box 160, Hong Kong. HD
$32.50 (Hong Kong dollars) per year soft cover; HK $50.00 hard
cover. (N/M)

Film Roumain/Romanian Film. Pictorial magazine. Articles on
films, with special emphasis on Romanian films. Extensive, detailed reviews of Romanian films. Sample titles of recent articles:
"On Top of the List of Favourites with the Public: The Historical
Film," "The Romanian Film in the World," "The Political Thril-
ler." 48 pages per issue. Published four to six times per year by
Cinema magazine, 25 Julius Fucik Street, Bucharest, Romania.
$1.00 per year. (M) Since 1966.

Florida State University Proceedings and Reports (formerly Florida
State University Slavic Papers). Interdisciplinary research and publication in the field of Slavic and East European studies with special emphasis on Yugoslavia and on comparative analysis. Announcements of the agendas of relevant conferences. Sample titles
of recent articles: "Workers in the Management of the Yugoslav
Economy," "Cultural Values in America and in East-Central Eu-

rope Today," "Theory of the Cost of Capital: Some Comparisons
between the American and Yugoslav Firm." About 85 to 125 pages
per issue. Published yearly by the Center for Yugoslav-American
Studies, Research, and Exchanges, Florida State University, Tal-
lahassee, Florida 32306. $3.00 per year. (N/M)

Florida State University Slavic Papers (see Florida State University
Proceedings and Reports).

For You from Czechoslovakia. Illustrated periodical. Information
on Czechoslovak ceramics, glass, jewelry, textiles, and so on.
Published quarterly by the Czechoslovak Chamber of Foreign
Trade, Prague, Czechoslovakia. Obtainable from Rapid, 13 ulice
28 rijna, Prague 1, Czechoslovakia. $10.00 per year. (M) Since
1961.

Foreign Affairs Bulletin. Concentrates primarily on international affairs and international trade relations of the German Democratic
Republic. Sample titles of recent articles: "Successful Develop-
ment of Relations with Norway," "Council for Mutual Economic
Assistance Met for Its 29th Session: Extracts from the Joint Com-
munique," "Meeting between L. I. Brezhnev and Erich Honecker."
Eight pages per issue. Published 35 times per year by the Press
Department of the Foreign Ministry of the German Democratic Re-
public, P.O. Box 101, 102 Berlin, German Democratic Republic.
Free. (M) Since 1973.

Foreign Affairs Research Papers Available. List of private and gov-
ernment-supported research papers added to the Foreign Affairs
Research Documentation Center of the U.S. Department of State.
Each entry includes name and business address (university connection, where applicable) of author; title of paper; type of meeting, place, and date at which paper was delivered; and number of
pages. Papers are listed in numerical order, under six main geographic headings, with "People's Republic of China" as a subdivision under "East Asia and Pacific Area" and with "Eastern Europe"
and "U.S.S.R." as subdivisions under "Europe." About 24 pages
per issue. Published monthly by the Office of External Research,
U.S. Department of State, Washington, D.C. Obtainable from
Superintendent of Documents, U.S. Government Printing Office,
Washington, D.C. 20402. $8.40 per year. (N/M)

Foreign Broadcast Information Service: Daily Report (see Daily Report [Foreign Broadcast Information Service]).

Foreign Trade. Pictorial magazine. Emphasis on the foreign trade
of the USSR. Some statistical tables. News of developments in

Soviet science and technology. Reports on international fairs and exhibitions in which the USSR participates. Relevant documents. Book reviews. Advertisements of products the USSR offers for sale abroad. Annual supplement (in Russian only) of complete statistical information on Soviet foreign trade. Declared purpose: "The journal deals with the theory and practice of Soviet economic relations with foreign countries, trade policy measures of the Soviet Union, problems of the development of foreign trade and other forms of economic cooperation, etc." Sample titles of recent articles: "Soviet Czechoslovak Cooperation," "Soviet Electric Locomotives in Finland," "Cooperation Between the CMEA Countries in Foreign Trade Accounting and Statistics." 64 pages per issue. Published monthly by the USSR Ministry of Foreign Trade, 4 Pudovkin Street, Moscow G-285, USSR. $13.50 per year. (M) Since 1975.

Foreign Trade Statistics (OECD) (see OECD Foreign Trade Statistics).

Fourth International. Official organ of the Trotskyist Fourth International. Articles on Marxist-Leninist theory and on events and developments of interest to Marxist-Leninists, analyzed from a Trotskyist point of view. Some illustrations; occasional book reviews. Publishers declare that the periodical "represents the unbroken chain of theoretical journals in the Bolshevik tradition, whose continuators were the Left Opposition led and inspired by Leon Trotsky." Sample titles of recent articles: "Marxism, Pragmatism and Revisionism," "Stalinism and the Liberation of Vietnam," "History of the Greek Civil War." About 45 to 55 pages per issue. Published quarterly by the International Committee of the Fourth International, 186 Chapham High Street, London SW4 7UG, England. 50 pence per issue; by subscription, 25 pence plus 11 pence postage per issue. (M) Since 1964.

Free China and Asia (see Asian Outlook).

Free China Review. Focus on economic, political, social, and cultural affairs, conditions, and developments in Taiwan and in mainland China. Also articles on Taiwan's struggle to remain an independent, non-Communist country. Documents; chronicle of day-by-day current events. Sample titles of recent articles dealing with mainland China: "New Upheaval Ahead," "Why Peiping Criticizes Confucius," "We Do Beschrei It" ("risking peace and freedom in a phony detente with the Maoists"). About 56 to 60 pages per issue. Published monthly. Obtainable from P.O. Box 337, Taipei, Taiwan, Republic of China. $3.00 per year; $5.00 for two years. (N/M) Since 1951.

GDR Review. Pictorial magazine concerned with all aspects of life
in the German Democratic Republic (GDR) and with international
political events and developments of interest to the GDR and to the
cause of communism. Special sections on "Friendship Mosaic,"
"Your Comment," and "Information at Readers' Request." Sample
titles of recent articles: "Solidarity with Vietnam, Now More than
Ever," "A New Civil Code in the GDR," "The Streets Are Safe at
Night." 64 pages per issue. Published monthly by the League of
the GDR for Friendship among the Peoples, Thälmannplatz 8-9,
108 Berlin, German Democratic Republic. Obtainable from Verlag
Zeit im Bild, Julian-Grimau-Allee, 801 Dresden, German Democratic Republic. $2.20 per year. (M) Since 1956.

Giai Phong. Pictorial magazine. Covers all aspects of life in Vietnam. By 1976, emphasis was still on the war in Vietnam, the victory, and the unification of North and South Vietnam. Sample titles
of recent articles: "The Liberated Areas: Truth and Friendship,"
"The Outstanding Women Workers from the South," "Culture Is
Also a Battle Front." About 30 pages per issue. Published monthly. Formerly obtainable from Giai Phong Pictorial, c/o Special
Representation of the RSVN (Republic of South Vietnam) in the
DRVN (Democratic Republic of Vietnam), Hanoi, Socialist Republic of Vietnam. (No other postunification address secured.) 60
cents per issue. (M)

Granma Weekly Review. Illustrated organ of the Central Committee
of the Communist party of Cuba. Articles on all aspects of life in
Cuba. Special emphasis on political, economic, and cultural news.
Section on "South of the Rio Grande," consisting of reports on and
analyses of conditions, events, and developments in other Latin
American countries. Sample titles of recent articles: "Notes on
the Draft Programmatic Platform of the Communist Party of Cuba
to Be Discussed in the 1st Congress," "The Hated Platt Amend-
ment," "The Escambray Theater Group of La Yaya." 12 pages per
issue. Published weekly at Avenue General Suarez y Territorial,
Plaza de la Revolucion "Jose Marti," Havana, Cuba. 10 cents per
issue. (M) Since 1966.

Holidays in Poland. Pictorial magazine aimed at promoting tourism
in Poland. Articles about tourist attractions. Also information on
Polish products of light industry offered for sale abroad and on
services available. Published twice a year by AGPOL—Foreign
Trade Publicity and Publishing Enterprise, POLEXPORTPRESS
Division, Marszalkowska 124, 00-950 Warsaw, Poland. $10.80
per year. (M) Since 1975.

Holidays in Romania. Pictorial magazine aimed at promoting tourism in Romania. Emphasis on the countryside, on cultural events, and on tourist attractions. Section entitled "Do You Speak Romanian?" which focuses on teaching sentences of use to tourists in Romania. Sample titles of recent articles: "Unknown Romania," "10 Foreigners at the Village Museum," "The Bucegi Natural Reservation." 24 pages per issue. Published quarterly by Romania's National Tourist Office, 7 Gen. Magheru Boulevard, Bucharest, Romania. Obtainable from Cartimex, 13 Decembre Street Nr. 3, P.O. Box 134-135, Bucharest, Romania. $10.00 per year. (M) Since 1958.

Hsinhua Selected News Items (see Hsinhua Weekly).

Hsinhua Weekly (formerly Hsinhua Selected News Items). News items from China's Hsinhua News Agency in English translation. Emphasis on political, economic, and social conditions, developments, and current events, primarily in China and the other socialist countries of Asia. Sample titles of recent articles: "People of Various Nationalities in China Warmly Celebrate May Day," "Trade Union in China—School for Educating Workers in Communist Ideas," "Vietnamese People's Brilliant Victory Hailed." About 32 to 44 pages per issue. Published weekly by the Hsinhua News Agency, Hong Kong Branch, 5 Sharp Street West, Hong Kong. Price not given. (M) Since 1966.

Hungarian Agricultural Review. Articles and abstracts of materials dealing with agriculture in Hungary. Published quarterly by Informacios Kozpont, P.O. Box 15, H-1253 Budapest 13, Hungary. Free on exchange for publications in the field of agricultural economics. (M) Since 1952.

Hungarian Book Review (formerly Books from Hungary). Illustrated magazine. Articles about the current Hungarian literary scene and other topics of interest to people concerned with Hungarian art and literature. Classified list of new Hungarian books; list of foreign-language books published in Hungary. Section on Hungarian authors published abroad. Book review articles. Sample titles of recent articles: "Looking Forward to the Book Fair in Frankfurt," "Diplomatic Papers on Hungary's Foreign Policy, 1936-45," "Great Music in a Nutshell." About 45 to 60 pages per issue. Published quarterly by the Hungarian Publishers and Booksellers' Association, Vorosmarty ter 1, Budapest V, Hungary. Obtainable from Kultura, P.O. Box 149, H-1389 Budapest 62, Hungary. $4.00 per year. (M) Since 1959.

Hungarian Cooperation. Emphasis on various aspects and activities of Hungarian cooperatives. Published twice a year by the National Council of Consumers' Cooperative Societies, Szabadsag ter 14, Budapest V, Hungary. Distributed primarily to cooperative organizations and institutions in 85 countries. Free. (M) Since 1958.

Hungarian Economy. Illustrated periodical in newspaper format. Emphasis on economic and business news from Hungary. Advertisements of commodities and groups of commodities Hungary offers for sale abroad; also advertisements of certain services (for instance designing or insurance). Sample titles of recent articles: "New System of Workers' Training," "New Features in Hungary's Economic Links with the Developing Countries," "Joint Companies—With Foreign Financial Interest." 36 pages per issue. Published quarterly at Blaha Lujza ter 3, 1959 Budapest VIII, Hungary. Editorial offices at V. Alhotmany u. 10, 1355 Budapest V, Hungary. Obtainable from Kultura, P.O. Box 149, H-1389 Budapest 62, Hungary. $9.00 per year. (M) Since 1972.

Hungarian Exporter (see New Hungarian Exporter).

Hungarian Foreign Trade. Illustrated magazine. Focus on developments in economics, industry, technology, science, culture, and travel in Hungary. Special emphasis on issues affecting, or relevant to, Hungary's international economic relations and particularly its export sector. Sample titles of recent articles: "What's New in Electronics?," "Cash Register Production in Cooperation," "Patentinform '75. Venue of Technical Novelties in Budapest." Published quarterly by the Hungarian Chamber of Commerce, Budapest, Hungary. Obtainable from Kultura, P.O. Box 149, H-1389 Budapest 62, Hungary. $9.00 per year. (M) Since 1949.

Hungarian Heavy Industries. Illustrated magazine. Some technical articles dealing with products, operations, techniques, and so on; some nontechnical, general articles focusing on Hungary's heavy industries. Advertisements of products Hungary's heavy industries offer for sale abroad. Sample titles of recent nontechnical articles: "Thirty Years of Hungarian Machine Industry," "The Significance of Cooperation in Industry," "Technical Novelties at Budapest International Spring Fair." Published quarterly by the Hungarian Chamber of Commerce. Editorial Office: P.O. Box 106, Budapest, Hungary. Obtainable from Kultura, P.O. Box 149, H-1389 Budapest 62, Hungary. $10.00 per year. (M) Since 1945.

Hungarian Law Review. Articles, documents, news, and reviews on Hungarian law. Sample titles of recent articles: "The Legal

Concept of the Hungarian Economic Reform and the Legal Status of the Socialist State Enterprise," "The New Regulation of Hungarian Copyright Law," "New Statutory Regulation of Consumers' Cooperatives." Averages 85 pages per issue. Published twice a year by the Association of Hungarian Jurists, Franklin Nyomda Szentkiralyi Utca 28, Budapest 8, Hungary. Obtainable from Kultura, P.O. Box 149, H-1389 Budapest 62, Hungary. Price not given; was $9.00 per year in 1970. (M) Since 1968.

Hungarian Music News. Declared purpose: "to inform readers about Hungarian musical life; events, institutions, guest performers, etc." Reviews of books, records, musical scores, and musical performances. Sample titles of recent articles: "The Academy of Music is 100 years old," "Ballet Events of the Budapest Musical Weeks," "Hungarian Composers Abroad." Six pages per issue. Published twice a month at Budapest Office of Music Competitions, V. Vorosmarty ter. 1, P.O. Box 80, H-1366, Budapest, Hungary. Free. (M) Since 1970.

Hungarian Musical Guide. Deals with musical life in Hungary. 130 to 140 pages per issue. Published annually by Budapest Office of Music Competitions, V. Vorosmarty ter. 1, P.O. Box 80, H-1366 Budapest, Hungary. Free. (M)

Hungarian Review. Pictorial magazine covering all aspects of life in Hungary but with a deemphasis on politics. Art reproductions; occasional short stories and poems; "Review of the Arts" (theater, films, exhibitions, books); stamp collectors' corner; recipes. Sample titles of recent articles: "How Workers' Families Spend Their Money," "The Illustrations of Miklos Borsos," "The Story of Two Gold Medals" (in table tennis). 24 pages per issue. Published monthly at Lenin Korut 9-11, 1073 Budapest, Hungary. Obtainable from Kultura, P.O. Box 149, H-1389 Budapest 62, Hungary. $6.00 per year. (M) Since 1955.

Hungarian Studies Newsletter. Brief descriptions of books and dissertations on Hungary; reports on relevant research in progress and on available scholarships. Some selected articles and other information of interest to scholars and students studying Hungary, such as "United States Hungarian Scientific Cooperation," "Long Awaited Reprints," "Portland State Summer Studies in Hungarian." Eight pages per issue. Published quarterly by Hungarian Research Center, American Hungarian Studies Foundation, P.O. Box 1084, New Brunswick, New Jersey 08903. $3.00 per year. (N/M) Since 1973.

Hungarian Trade Union News. Illustrated magazine. Focus on economic, political, social, and cultural conditions, events, and developments in Hungary (and, to a much lesser extent, elsewhere). Emphasis on items of interest to Hungarian workers in general and to trade union members in particular. Letters to the editor; questions by readers and replies by the editors. Sample titles of recent articles: "Support for Physical Training—Part of the Trade Union's Protection of Members' Interests," "A [Hungarian] Working Class Family in 1941 and in 1975," "Is the Effect of the Capitalist Economic Crisis Being Felt in Hungary?" About 24 to 32 pages per issue. Published monthly by the Central Council of Hungarian Trade Unions, Dozsa Gyorgi ut 84/B, 1415 Budapest VI, Hungary. Price not given. (M)

Hungarian Travel Magazine. Pictorial magazine aimed at promoting tourism in Hungary. Published quarterly at Lenin Krt. 9-11, H-1073, Budapest, Hungary. Obtainable from Kultura P.O. Box 149, H-1389 Budapest 62, Hungary. $7.00 per year. (M)

Hungarofilm Bulletin. Hungarian film magazine. Film reviews. Text in English, French, and German. Published five times per year by Hungarofilm, Bathory 4. 10, Budapest 5, Hungary. Free. (M) Since 1965.

Hungaropress Economic Information. Latest economic and business developments in Hungary. Section on economic life in Hungary, on new investment projects, on international economic relations, specific export-import agreements, agriculture, inventions, exhibitions and fairs, and so on. Sample titles of recent articles: "Hungary's National Bank's Policy in 1975," "New 400 Kilovolt Power Transmission Line Linking Hungary and Czechoslovakia," "Hungarian-Italian Agreement for the Barter of Chemicals." About eight to nine pages per issue. Published every two weeks by the Press and Information Department, Hungarian Chamber of Commerce, Lengyel u. 6, 1054 Budapest V, Hungary. Distributed free to the press and a small mailing list. (M)

Hungary. Comprehensive survey, with background material, documents, and statistical data on Hungary. A recent issue consisted of the following main sections: "State Administration," "Political and Social Organizations," "Home Affairs," "International Relations—Foreign Affairs," "Economy," "The National Income and Where It Goes," "The Budget and the National Economic Plan," "The System of Management of Hungarian Economy," "Social Welfare," "Culture—Art," "Sports," and "Events with Reference to

Hungary" (this last section covering visits by VIPs and delegations to and from Hungary). 70 pages per issue. Published twice a year by Hungarian News Agency MTI, Fem Utca 5-7, H-1426 Budapest, Hungary. $15.00 per year. (M) Since 1969.

IASP Journals of Translations. Translations, primarily of scholarly articles from original sources. Declared purpose: "to reflect developments . . . and to be of most interest to those professionally concerned with the field."
The following IASP (International Arts and Sciences Press) journals are included in this index.

Monthly

Problems of Economics (USSR)
Soviet Education

Quarterly

Chinese Economic Studies
Chinese Education
Chinese Law and Government
Chinese Sociology and Anthropology
Chinese Studies in History
Chinese Studies in Philosophy
Eastern European Economics
Matekon (Mathematical Economics, USSR)
Soviet and East European Foreign Trade
Soviet Law and Government
Soviet Review
Soviet Sociology
Soviet Statutes and Decisions
Soviet Studies in History
Soviet Studies in Literature
Soviet Studies in Philosophy

All IASP journals are published by the International Arts and Sciences Press, 901 North Broadway, White Plains, New York 10603. For detailed descriptions, see separate entries under journal titles in this index.

In Soviet Ukraine. Articles on the Ukraine with emphasis on environment, culture, and social issues. Short stories. Section of brief items of current "Events and Facts." Sample titles of recent articles: "The Mironivka Bountiful Ear of Wheat," "Soviet Guaran-

tees," "Not a Day Passes without a Song." Published monthly by
the Ukrainian Society for Friendship and Cultural Relations with
Foreign Countries, Kiev, USSR. Price not given. (M)

Indeks (see Index).

Index. Review of economic statistics on all aspects of the Yugoslav
economy. Included, for instance, are detailed statistics on manu-
facturing, mining, trade, tourism, the labor force, and finance.
Published as Indeks in Serbo-Croatian, accompanied by an English-
language insert (Index), about 24 pages. Published monthly by the
Federal Institute for Statistics, Kneza Milosa 20, 11000 Belgrade,
Yugoslavia. $20.00 per year. (M)

Index to Pravda. English-language guide to Pravda, official newspaper of the Communist party of the Soviet Union. Divided into two
parts: "Subjects" and "Personal Names." Entry statements cover
both foreign and domestic affairs. Extensive cross-references
lead user to related or more specific subjects. All Party and government affairs, economic news, local news, and events of significance are indexed under both the appropriate general headings and
a geographical heading. "Personal Names" section, where the ca-
reers of Soviet officals may be followed in great detail, includes
not only national leaders but also those at the district and plant-
manager levels. Each entry provides a capsulized description of
the article along with the day, month, and year of the Pravda issue
and the page and column where the information or name appears.
About 52 pages per issue. Published monthly by the American Association for the Advancement of Slavic Studies, Index to Pravda,
2043 Millikin Road, Columbus, Ohio 43210. Subscribers also receive a Cumulated Annual Index. Subscribers have option of receiving Index in printed form or on four-by-six-inch microfiche;
microfiche subscribers have further option of receiving the Cumulated Annual Index on either microfiche or paper. $225.00 per
year. (M; N/M) Since 1975.

Indochina Solidarity Committee, Newsletter. Reports on the socialist
countries of Indochina. Some illustrations and cartoons. Sample
titles of recent articles: "Cambodia: Triumphant Song of Self-Re-
liance," "Building the New South Vietnam: A Life with a Purpose,"
"Southeast Asia after the Victories." About 33 pages per issue.
Published by the Indochina Solidarity Committee, 41 Union Square
West, Room 629, New York, N.Y. 10003. $3.00 per year; $10.00
to institutions; Free to prisoners. (M) Since 1974.

Information Bulletin. Speeches, official statements, documents, congress and conference reports, and so on from Communist and

workers' parties around the world and from governments of socialist countries. Occasional translations of articles from the Communist press in socialist and nonsocialist countries. Section entitled "In Brief" featuring country-by-country reports of events
(public rallies, important publications, treaties, and so on) of interest to Marxist-Leninists. Sample titles of recent articles: "The
21st Convention of the Communist Party USA," "National Emergen-
cy and Our Tasks: Resolution of the Central Executive, Communist Party of India," "Plenum of Central Committee, Hungarian
Socialist Workers' Party." 56 pages per issue. Published twice
a month by Progress Books, 487 Adelaide Street West, Toronto,
Ontario, Canada. Free to subscribers of World Marxist Review,
described separately below; 10 cents per issue to nonsubscribers.
(M)

Information Bulletin, Narodowy Bank Polski (see Narodowy Bank Polski: Information Bulletin).

Information Moscow. Handbook for foreigners visiting Moscow. Lists
addresses, phone numbers, and in some cases other relevant information (such as opening and closing hours) for government offices, Soviet organizations, theaters, concert halls, motion picture theaters, libraries, parks, restaurants, shops, services
(rent-a-car, insurance, legal counsel, travel services, and so
on), foreign representatives (airline, business, bank, and so on),
members of the diplomatic corps, and so on in Moscow. Also section on consulates in Leningrad and on hotels, restaurants, shops,
and so on in Helsinki. Published twice a year by Jennifer Louis,
Leninsky Prospect 45, Apt. 426, Moscow, USSR. $4.30 per is-
sue. (M)

Insight: Soviet Jews. Analysis of all aspects of the Jewish problem in
the USSR with emphasis on alleged anti-Semitism and discrimination against Jews. Declared purpose: "to look beyond the day to
day news in order to give a coherent picture of Soviet-Jewish developments." Each issue devoted to one single topic, generally
contained in one single article. Sample titles of recent articles:
"Anti-Zionism and Anti-Semitism," "Jews, Dissent and the Future," "The Soviet Version (1): An Answer to Critics, (2): Jews
and Judaism." Eight pages per issue. Published monthly by European Jewish Publications, Ltd., 31 Percy Street, London WIP
9FG, England. $30.00 per year. (N/M) Since 1975.

International Affairs (Moscow). * Covers economic and political affairs, conditions, and developments in the USSR and in other countries. Emphasis on international relations, including the history
of international relations and contemporary international law. Sections on "Foreign Policy and the Struggle of Ideologies," "Facts
and Figures," "Exchange of Opinions." Reports on international
organizations and conferences. Book reviews. Declared purpose:
to be "a journal of political analysis [that] examines the foreign
policy of the USSR and other states." Sample titles of recent articles: "Restructuring of International Economic Relations," "The
American Way of Life: Promise and Reality," "The World Oceans
and International Law." Published monthly by the All Union Society "Znaniye," 14 Gorokhovsky Pereulok, Moscow K-64, USSR.
$5.50 per year. (M) Since 1955.

International Bulletin (see Modern China Studies: International Bulletin).

International Review of East-West Trade. Semitechnical magazine
aimed at presenting Western technology and processes, production
techniques, and marketing and management practices to the socialist countries. Averages at least 24 pages per issue. Published
every two months by Symposium Press, 245 Mamaroneck Avenue,
White Plains, New York 10605. $10.00 per year. (N/M) Since
1970.

International Review of History and Political Science. Articles on
history and on political affairs and developments in countries a-
round the world. Many articles deal with nonsocialist countries,
but contributions on socialist countries are featured regularly.
Sample titles of recent articles dealing with socialist countries:
"Toward the Comparative Study of the Process of Modernization
in the Soviet Union," "The Historical Development of the Mongolian People's Republic," "The Changing Role of the Communist
Party in Hungary." About 100 to 150 pages per issue. Published
quarterly by Review Publications, Meerut-2, India. $8.00 per
year. (N/M) Since 1964.

Interpressgrafik. Pictorial magazine. Emphasis on graphic art in
Hungary. Declared purpose: "to provide a unique forum to graphic
artists, photographers and typographers of the socialist countries.

---

*Not to be confused with International Affairs (London)

The special issues of the periodical give an overall picture of the newest aspirations and results in the field of graphics concerning the countries covered." Text in several languages, including German, Russian, and English. Art reproductions. Advertisements of items Hungary offers for sale abroad. Sample titles of recent articles: "The Graphic Architecture of the Bulgarian Press," "Animated Cartoons in the Service of Progress," "On Changes in Book Typography." Averages 95 pages per issue. Published quarterly by the Interpress Publishing House (which belongs to the International Association of Journalists), Budapest, Hungary. Obtainable from Kultura, P.O. Box 149, H-1389 Budapest, Hungary. $16.00 per year. (M) Since 1970.

Issues and Studies. Emphasis primarily on the problems of the People's Republic of China and secondarily on other international problems. Sections on current affairs; documents; descriptions of personalities; chronicle of events. Published monthly by the Institute of International Relations, P.O. Box 1189, Taipei, Taiwan, Republic of China. $14.00 per year. (N/M) Since 1964.

Jews and the Jewish People. A selection of news items and of articles concerning Jews who reside in the Soviet Union, translated from the Soviet daily and periodical press. Published every two months by Contemporary Jewish Library Ltd., 31 Percy Street, London W1, England. Price not given; was $2.00 per issue in 1970. (M) Since 1962.

Jews in the USSR. Information Bulletin. Focus on the position of Jews in the Soviet Union with emphasis on alleged discrimination against Jews. Sample titles of recent articles: "Dr. Shtern Transferred to Hard Labour," "Kishinev Jews' Plea for Theatre," "Kharkov Jews Fight Back." Averages 4-6 pages per issue. Published weekly by Contemporary Jewish Library, 31 Percy Street, London, WIP 9FG, England. $40.00 per year. (N/M) Since 1972.

Joint Economic Committee: Papers and Hearings. Papers submitted to, and hearings before, the Joint Economic Committee of the Congress of the United States. Emphasis primarily on economic, and to a somewhat lesser extent political and military, conditions and developments in the Soviet Union, China, and East Europe. Sample titles of recent volumes: Soviet Economic Prospects for the Seventies; China: A Reassessment of the Economy; Reorientation and Commercial Relations of the Economies of Eastern Europe. Sample titles of articles in the last volume mentioned: "Population and Labor Force in Eastern Europe: 1950-1996," "Education and Economic Growth: The Postwar Experience in Hungary," "Eastern

Europe: The Political Context." Length varies from under 100 to over 750 pages. Published irregularly, on the average at least once a year, by the Joint Economic Committee of the Congress of the United States. Obtainable from Superintendent of Documents, U.S. Government Printing Office, Washington, D.C. 20402. Prices vary, recently from 60 cents to over $6.00 per volume. (N/M)

Joint Publications Research Service Reports (see JPRS Reports).

Journal of Comparative Economics (see ACES Bulletin).

Journal of Contemporary Asia. Interdisciplinary journal primarily devoted to politics, economics, and ideology in Asia. Special emphasis on Marxism, class relations, the class struggle, and the achievements of socialism, wherever applicable. Documents, largely those issued by Communist and workers' parties and organizations and their leaders, such as "Statement of the Communist Party of Burma on the Death of Thakin Zin and Thakin Chit," "Special Communique by the Provisional Revolutionary Government of South Vietnam on Two Years of the Paris Agreement," "Kim Il Sung on Imperialism." Book reviews. Sample titles of recent articles: "Marxism in India," "Economic Comparison of North and South Korea," "8 Invincible Strength [sic] of Vietnam-Cambodian Solidarity." About 120 to 160 pages per issue. Published quarterly at P.O. Box 49010, Stockholm 49, Sweden. $12.00 per year for individuals; $20.00 for institutions and libraries; $30.00 for government agencies and business firms. (M; N/M) Since 1970.

Journal of Croatian Studies. Interdisciplinary journal covering topics in a wide variety of disciplines relevant primarily to Croatia and secondarily to other parts of Yugoslavia. Some emphasis on Croatian literature, culture, and history. Occasional translations of Croatian short stories and poems. Announcements and reports of activities of the Croatian Academy of America. Book reviews. Sample titles of recent articles: "Some Specific Themes of Contemporary Slovenian Poetry," "The Evolution of the Economic System of Yugoslavia and the Economic Position of Croatia Today" (translated from an article originally published in Zagreb), "Geographic Manuscripts Concerning Croatia in the British Museum." Varies in length from under 150 to over 200 pages per issue. Published annually by the Croatian Academy of America, P.O. Box 1767, Grand Central Station, New York, N.Y. 10017. $10.00 per year; free to members of the Croatian Academy. (M; N/M)

Journal of East and West Studies. Interdisciplinary journal concerned
with East-West and with North Korea-South Korea problems.
Primary emphasis on Korea and China, but not all articles deal
with communism or Communist countries. Sample titles of recent
articles: "Peking's Ideological Influence on North Korea," "Re-
flections on the Political Economy of Planning: The Case of Korea,"
"The Racial Factor in the Sino-Soviet Relationship." About 140 to
160 pages per issue. Published twice a year by the Institute of
East and West Studies, Yonsei University, # 134 Shinchon-dong,
Seodaemoon-gu, Seoul, Republic of Korea. $7.00 per year. (N/M)
Since 1973.

Journal of Korean Affairs. Reports and analyses of current developments in North and South Korea. Day-by-day "Chronicle of Events"
as recorded by the North Korean press and radio. Declared purpose: "(1) Objective research and analysis in the field of Korean
affairs for use by academic communities and educational institutions; (2) dissemination of authoritative information on Korean affairs to non-specialist individuals and organizations, and (3) establishment of a forum for professional discussion on Korean affairs."
Sample titles of recent articles: "The Citizenship Status of Koreans
in Pre-revolutionary Russia and the Early Years of the Soviet Regime," "South-North Dialogue: A North Korean Peace Offensive?,"
"Report on the DPRK [Democratic People's Republic of Korea] Budget for 1974-75." About 50 to 60 pages per issue. Published quarterly by the Research Institute on Korean Affairs, 8555 16th street,
Suite 703, Silver Spring, Maryland 20910. $8.00 per year; $15.00
for two years. (M; N/M) Since 1971.

Journal of Southeast Asia and the Far East (see Asia Quarterly).

Journal of the Moscow Patriarchate. Illustrated religious periodical
of the Russian Orthodox Church. Articles and reports on church
life, church affairs, sermons, theology, ecumenia, and so on.
Reviews of relevant publications. Sample titles of recent articles:
"The Foundations of Christian Morals," "Theological Conversations between the US and USSR Religious Leaders in Moscow,"
"Holy Easter in the Patriarchal Cathedral." About 80 pages per
issue. Published monthly by the Publishing Department of the
Moscow Patriarchate, P.O. Box 624, Moscow G-435, USSR. $1.00
per year. (M; N/M)

Journal of the US-USSR Trade and Economic Council. Reports on activities of the US-USSR Trade and Economic Council (a nonprofit
organization with offices in New York and Moscow), on U.S.-USSR
business transactions, and on related subjects of interest to those

who engage in commerce between the two countries. Declared purpose of the journal and of the US-USSR Trade and Economic Council: "To strengthen the commercial and economic ties between the
United States and the Soviet Union by encouraging trade." A special section on "Business in the USSR" is devoted to offering "how-
to" knowledge on such topics as industrial cooperation, trade regulations, shipping, industrial property protection, banking and financing, and operating offices in the Soviet Union. Sample titles
of recent articles: "Financing Soviet-American Trade through
1980," "Agreements: A Tested Form of Cooperation with the
USSR," "Soviet Resources on a Participation Basis." About 32
pages per issue. Published every two months by the US-USSR
Trade and Economic Council, 280 Park Avenue, New York, N. Y.
10017. Free to member-companies of the council; nonmembers
should inquire. (N/M)

Journal of Yugoslav Foreign Trade. Pictorial magazine. Focus on
Yugoslav exports, imports, industry, mining, agriculture, finance,
tourist information, and related items. Advertisements of products Yugoslavia wants to export. Published quarterly by Export
Press, Francuska br. 27, Belgrade 11000, Yugoslavia. $8.00
per year. (M) Since 1954.

JPRS Reports. Translations by the Joint Publications Research Service (JPRS, an agency of the U.S. government) from foreign newspapers, magazines, journals, and so on. Most of these periodicals
come from socialist countries; about half of them from the Soviet
Union. All social science disciplines are covered, but about half
of the reports are in scientific and technical fields. Reports vary
greatly in length, from just a few to 60, 70, 80, and more pages
per report. In all, JPRS publishes about 200,000 pages of these
translations-reports a year.

In the detailed description given below, the reports on Africa, the Near East, and Latin America have been omitted since
they deal only marginally with issues related to communism; also
omitted are reports in strictly scientific and technical fields, such
as USSR: Metereology and Hydrology or USSR/Eastern Europe:
Bio-Medical Sciences. Note that subscription prices given below
are estimates; exact prices depend upon the total amount of material actually published under the respective headings.

People's Republic of China

Political, sociological, economic, military, and scientific and
technological information. Published irregularly, two to four reports per month. $88.00 per year.

USSR

Political and Sociological Affairs. Government and party structure, policy and problems, law and social regulations, education, and cultural and social aspects of Soviet life. Published irregularly, 10 to 12 times per month. $180.00 per year.

Military Affairs. Soviet military and civil defense establishments, leadership, doctrine, policy, planning, political affairs, organization, and equipment. Published irregularly, nine to ten times per month. $160.00 per year.

Translations from Kommunist. Political, economic, military, and social developments in the USSR, and their relationship to other countries. All articles translated from the Soviet party organ Kommunist. Published 18 times per year. $40.00 per year.

USA: Economics, Politics, Ideology. Articles by Soviet public figures, Americanologists, and others on Soviet-American relations and on political, military, economic, scientific, technological, and other aspects of life in the United States. All articles taken from the Soviet monthly USA. Published monthly. $28.00 per year.

Problems of the Far East. Articles by Soviet public figures and experts on Soviet relations with China and other Asian countries. Focus on political, military, economic, scientific, and technological aspects of life in China and other Asian countries. All articles taken from the Soviet quarterly Problems of the Far East. Published quarterly. $20.00 per year.

Economic Affairs. Recent administrative plans, changes, and policy trends. Items on the state of the national economy; significant and representative comments and statistics on principal industrial sectors. Published irregularly, 8 to 12 times per month. $175.00 per year.

Agriculture. Trends and policy at the national and republic levels, plans and plan fulfillments, production statistics, technological achievements and shortcomings, and agricultural investments, administration, and management. Information at lower levels included when considered indicative of trends or innovations. Published irregularly, nine to ten times per month. $150.00 per year.

Industrial Affairs. Development and productivity of the automotive and tractor industry, chemical industry and chemical machinery output, electronic and precision equipment activities, and metal-working equipment field. Published irregularly, five to seven times per month. $95.00 per year.

Resources. Electric power, fuels, and related equipment; labor and trade union activities; metallurgy and mineral fields; fishing industry and marine resources, water resources, and environmental degradation. Published irregularly, six to eight times per month. $135.00 per year.

Trade and Services. Transportation and communication; construction, construction machinery, building materials, consumer goods, domestic trade, and international economic relations. Published irregularly, 10 to 12 times per month. $275.00 per year.

Soviet Public Health. Public health measures, immunology, general hygiene, new health laws and special orders, and the organization of the USSR Ministry of Health. All articles taken from the Soviet monthly Soviet Public Health. Published monthly. $28.00 per year.

Eastern Europe

Economic and Industrial Affairs. Economic theory, organization, planning, and management; major agreements on, and development of, trade within Council for Mutual Economic Aid (CMEA) and outside the bloc; aspects of materials, services, machine, electronics, and precision equipment industries; concepts and attainments in agriculture, forestry, and the food industry. Published irregularly, 12 to 18 times per month. $720.00 per year.

Political, Sociological, and Military Affairs. Official Party and government pronouncements and writings on significant domestic political developments; general sociological problems and developments in such areas as demography, manpower, public health and welfare, education, and mass organizations; military and civil defense, organization, theory, budget, and hardware. Published irregularly, 12 to 15 times per month. $350.00 per year.

Western Europe

Political-economic information on Western European energy, finance, and trade policy matters as well as developments and trends in the doctrine, programs, and problems of the major Communist parties, including their relations with Communist parties outside the Western European area. Published irregularly, one to two times per week. $150.00 per year. (M; N/M)

South and East Asia

Political, economic, sociological, and technological developments, with considerable emphasis on Cambodia, Laos, Indonesia, and Japan. Published irregularly, about five times per month. $80.00 per year.

Mongolia

Political, sociological, economic, and technological developments as reported primarily in Mongolian publications. Published irregularly, one to two times per month. $44.00 per year.

North Korea

Political, economic, and sociological events and developments. Published irregularly, three to four times per month. $54.00 per year.

Vietnam

Military, political, sociological, economic, and technical developments selected from North and South Vietnamese and foreign newspapers and periodicals. Includes translation of "HOC Tap." Published irregularly, about three times per week. $262.00 per year. (M; N/M)

World

Environmental Quality. Articles and press commentary on environmental pollution and its effects, pollution control technology, organizations, and programs, primarily of the USSR, East Europe, and Japan. Published irregularly, two to three times per month. $81.50 per year. (M; N/M)

JPRS Reports are published by the Joint Publications Research Service, 1000 North Glebe Road, Arlington, Virginia 22201. Obtainable from U.S. Department of Commerce, National Technical Information Service (NTIS), 5235 Port Royal Road, Springfield,

Virginia 22151. JPRS Reports are also available on microfiche or microfilm; offered with this service is a monthly printed index to UPRS translations and an annual cumulative index on microfiche or microfilm. These services can be obtained from the Micro Photo Division of Bell & Howell, Old Munsfield Road, Wooster, Ohio 44691. Price information and complete details on request. (M, unless otherwise indicated in the description above.) Since 1957 to government agencies; since 1963 to the public.

Jugoslawische Touristenzeitung/Yugoslav Tourist News. Published monthly by Turisticka Stampa, Knez Mihailova 21, Belgrade, Yugoslavia. $3.00 per year. (M) Since 1958. (No further information procured.)

Korea Focus. Emphasis on economic, social, political, and cultural conditions and developments in North Korea. Some pictures; book reviews; letters to the editor. Declared purpose: "to promote lasting friendship leading to relaxation of tension, advancement of peaceful co-existence and detente, based on mutual understanding between the people of Korea and the USA." Declared by the publishers to be "non-Marxist but definitely not anti-Marxist, anti-Communist, or anti-Soviet." Sample titles of recent articles: "The Democratic Republic of Korea—Socialism and Modernization in ·One Generation," "A Transformation in Education," "The DPRK's Reunification Efforts." About 60 pages per issue. Published every two months by the American-Korean Friendship and Information Center, 160 Fifth Avenue, New York, N. Y. 10010. $5.00 per year. (N/M) Since 1971.

Korea Today. Primary emphasis on the political, social, and economic progress of North Korea, on North Korea's relations with other countries, and on the future unification of North and South Korea. Occasional pictures. Sample titles of recent articles: "All Efforts to Attain the Goal of Eight Million Tons of Grain," "Joint Communique of Democratic People's Republic of Korea and People's Republic of China," "US Imperialism—Ignitor of Aggressive War in Korea." About 45 to 55 pages per issue. Published monthly by the Foreign Languages Publishing House, Pyongyang, Democratic People's Republic of Korea. Price not given; was $2.00 per year in 1970. (M)

Labour in Exile. Articles on labor, labor unions, workers' living and working conditions in East Europe, and related topics. Published every two months by the International Centre of Free Trade Unionists in Exile, 24 B Clifton Gardens, London W9, England. $2.40 per year. (N/M) Since 1949.

Latvian Information Bulletin. Reports on events in the Soviet Union and on political statements, resolutions, and developments in the West that are of special interest to Latvians. Focus on demands for independence for Latvia and also for Estonia and Lithuania. Sample titles of recent articles: "A Tale of Latvian Slave Laborers in the USSR," "U.S. Congress Unanimously Adopts House Resolution 864 Condemning Soviet Annexation of the Baltic States," "Solzhenitsyn and the Baltic Nations." Published quarterly by the Latvian Legation, 4325 Seventeenth Street, N.W., Washington, D.C. 20011. Free (N/M)

Law in Eastern Europe. Series of volume-length studies and symposiums on varying aspects of the legal system of East European, and occasionally other, socialist countries. Sample titles of recent volumes: "Governmental Tort Liability in the Soviet Union, Bulgaria, Czechoslovakia, Hungary, Poland, Romania and Yugoslavia," "Polish Civil Law," "Codification in the Communist World." Varies in length from under 100 to almost 500 pages per volume. Published irregularly, on the average about once a year, by the Documentation Office for East European Law, University of Leyden, 82 Rapenburg, Leyden, The Netherlands. Obtainable from A. W. Sijthoff, P.O. Box 26, Leyden, The Netherlands. Prices vary from under 10 to over 50 Dutch florins per volume. (N/M)

Left Curve. Illustrated experimental art magazine. Focus on theoretical and practical issues concerning art and revolution, primarily from a Marxist point of view. Covers all art forms from experimental to traditional with emphasis on original material of active contemporary artists, writers, and critics, both in the United States and abroad. Reproductions of paintings, graphics, photos, and poems. Book reviews; letters to the editor. Sample titles of recent articles: "The Cultural Revolution in the Philippines," "Exhaustion of an Ideology: Bankruptcy of 'Modernism,'" "Truth Is a Convincing Answer" (conversation with three Vietnamese women writers). 58 to 104 pages per issue. Published three times a year at 1016 Greenwich Street, San Francisco, California 94133. $4.50 per year for individuals; $6.50 for institutions. (M) Since 1974.

Lithuania Today. Pictorial magazine covering economic, political, social, and cultural conditions and developments in Lithuania, the history of the Lithuanian people, and Lithuania's relations with foreign countries. Art reproductions; occasional poems. Sample titles of recent articles: "Lithuanian Industry: Past, Present, and

Future," "Vilnius: Thirtieth Anniversary of Liberation," "Mikalojus Konstantinas Ciurlionis: The 100th Birthday of the Great Lithuanian Painter and Composer." 48 to 100 pages per issue. Published once or twice a year by the Lithuanian Society for Friendship and Cultural Relations with Foreign Countries, Kosciuskos 36, Vilnius, Lithuania, USSR. Free. (M)

Lituanus. Emphasis on Lithuanian history, politics, and art. Occasional documents, poems, and book reviews. Described by the publishers as "a journal of arts and sciences, dedicated to the presentation and examination of all questions pertaining to the countries and peoples of the Baltic States, particularly Lithuania." Sample titles of recent articles: "The Decision of the Lithuanan Government to Accept the Soviet Ultimatum of June 14, 1940," "The Chronicles of the Lithuanian Catholic Church Continue Publication," "Lithuanian Folk Art Motifs at St. Casimir Lithuanian Cemetery in Chicago, Ill." 80 pages per issue. Published quarterly by the Lituanus Foundation, 6621 South Troy, Chicago, Illinois 60629. $8.00 per year. (N/M) Since 1954.

Marketing in Hungary. Focus on marketing, market research, export-import, and related business and economic subjects in Hungary. Discussion of topics relevant to the establishment of commercial relations with enterprises in foreign countries. Practical advice for foreigners interested in business connections with Hungarian firms. Sample titles of recent articles: "Hungary's Trade Policy Towards Advanced Capitalist Countries," "Transfer of Hungarian Technology of Developing Countries," "International Cooperation in the Hungarian Building Industry." Published quarterly by the Hungarian Chamber of Commerce and the Institute for Economic and Market Research, V. Lenyel u. 6, Budapest, Hungary. Obtainable from Kultura, P.O. Box 149, H-1389 Budapest 62, Hungary. $20.00 per year. (M) Since 1970.

Marxism Today. Official organ of the Communist party of Great Britain. Articles on Marxist-Leninist theory and on practical current problems. Section of "Editorial Comments" dealing with current problems. Sample titles of recent articles: "The Concept of Stratum in the Class Analysis of Advanced Capitalist Societies," "What the Communists Want for France," "Some Thoughts on the Party's Policy Towards Prices, Wages, and Incomes." 32 pages per issue. Published monthly by the Communist party of Great Britain, 16 King Street, London WC3E 8HS, England. Obtainable from Central Books Ltd., 37 Gray's Inn Road, London WC1X 8PS, England. £4.27 per year. (M)

Marxist Studies. Published quarterly at 16s Holmdale Road, London NW6, England. $1.80 per year. (U) Since 1969. (No further information procured.)

Matekon (formerly Mathematical Studies in Economics and Statistics in the USSR and Eastern Europe). Unabridged translations of articles in the area of mathematical economics taken from Soviet and East European academic sources, primarily scholarly journals and collections of articles published in book form. Sample titles of recent articles: "Calculation and Analysis of Interindustry Proportions in the National Economy of the USSR," "Industry Price Levels and the Norm of Effectiveness in the System of Optimal Planning," "The Mathematical Model of Reproduction of Karl Marx and V. I. Lenin." Averages over 100 pages per issue. Published quarterly by the International Arts and Sciences Press, 901 North Broadway, White Plains, New York 10603. $70.00 per year for institutions; $20.00 for individuals associated with subscribing institutions. (M) Since 1964.

Mathematical Studies in Economics and Statistics in the USSR and Eastern Europe (see Matekon).

Miorita: A Journal of Romanian Studies. Emphasis on Romanian culture and history. Book reviews. Sample titles of recent articles: "Romanian House Decoration in Stucco," "Two Legends: Manole and Vortigern's Tower," "Celtic Death Rituals in Romanian Traditions." About 40 to 60 pages per issue. Published twice a year by the New Zealand Romanian Cultural Association, c/o English Department, University of Waikato, Hamilton, New Zealand. $4.00 per year for individuals; $5.00 for institutions; $7.50 and $9.00, respectively, for two years. (N/M) Since 1974.

Modern China. Focus on political, economic, social, and educational aspects of life in China. Sample titles of recent articles: "Analyzing the Twentieth-Century Countryside: Revolutionaries versus Western Scholarship," "The Great Leap Forward Reconsidered," "Women under Kuomingtag Rule: Variations of the Feminist Mystique." About 100 to 125 pages per issue. Published quarterly by Sage Publications, 275 South Beverly Drive, Beverly Hills, California 90212. $20.00 per year for institutions; $12.00 for professionals and teachers; $10.00 for full-time college and university students. (N/M) Since 1975.

Modern China Series. Booklets, each dealing with some aspect of life in China or of China's socialist system. Sample titles of recent booklets: Education in China, The Women's Movement in Chi-

na, Economic Management in China. Varying lengths, recently
from 40 to 112 pages per booklet. Published irregularly, about
two per year, by Anglo-Chinese Educational Institute, 24 Warren
Street, London W1P 5DG, England. Most booklets $1.50 each;
some $2.50. (M; N/M)

Modern China Studies: International Bulletin. Reports on postgraduate
research on China, subdivided by discipline. Items listed contain
researcher's name, address, university connection, project title,
and a brief summary of the project. Smaller sections on movements of faculty members, conferences, and bibliographies. A-
bout 85 pages per issue. Published yearly by China Quarterly,
Contemporary China Institute, School of Oriental and African Studies, London University, Malet Street, London WCIE 7HP, England. $5.00 per year for individuals; $10.00 for institutions.
(N/M) Since 1970.

Mongolian Society Bulletin (see Mongolian Studies).

Mongolian Society Newsletter (see Mongolian Studies).

Mongolian Studies (formerly Mongolian Society Newsletter; supersedes
Mongolian Society Bulletin). Interdisciplinary journal devoted to the
study of Mongols and their impact on history, from the 12th century to the present. Review articles, book reviews, translations
of modern short stories and of literary documents. Sample titles
of recent articles: "The Seven Jewels in Mongol Literature,"
"Mongol Rule in East Asia, 12th-14th Centuries: An Assessment
of Recent Soviet Scholarship," "Social Change on a Mongol Cooperative." 100 to 175 pages per issue. Published annually by The
Mongolian Society, Inc., P.O. Box 606, Bloomington, Indiana
47401. $10.00 per year; $5.00 for students. (N/M)

Monitoring Report (see B.B.C. Monitoring Service).

Monthly Bulletin of Statistics. Statistical information with emphasis
on economic data, including such topics as population, food, trade,
production, finance, and national income. Covers over 185 countries, including all the socialist countries. About 300 pages per
issue. Published monthly by the United Nations. Obtainable from
United Nations Publications, LX 2300, New York, N.Y. 10017.
$70.00 per year. (M; N/M) Since 1947.

Monthly Review. Analyses of events, conditions, and developments
of interest to Marxist-Leninists. Articles deal with socialist and
nonsocialist countries. Declared by the publishers to be an "Independent Socialist Magazine"; but many of the articles are reflective

of the Chinese interpretation of Marxism-Leninism. Special section entitled "Review of the Month." Book reviews. Sample titles of recent articles: "The U.S.-Cuban Policy Debate," "Class and Class Conflict in Africa," "Bangladesh: The Internationalization of Counter-revolution." 64 pages per issue. Published monthly by the Monthly Review Press, 62 West 14th Street, New York, N.Y. 10011. $9.00 per year; $7.00 for students. (M) Since 1949.

Moscow Narodny Bank Limited: Quarterly Review. Financial review concerned primarily with analyses of current developments in the foreign exchange and gold markets and with the international monetary system. Occasional articles on economic conditions per se and on related macroeconomic topics. Statistical tables cover mainly current and very recent conditions and developments. Sample titles of recent articles: "Monetary Policy and Inflation in an Open Economy," "1975: Crisis Year for the Western Economy," "Gold: The Free Market Price of Gold; Production, Supply and Demand Considerations; Implications of Gold Sales by the United States and the Monetary Role of Gold." About 42 pages per issue. Published quarterly by the (Soviet-owned) Moscow Narodny Bank Limited, P.O. Box 26, 24/32 King William Street, London EC4P 4JS, England. Free on a limited circulation basis. (M) Since 1974.

Moscow News. Illustrated newspaper covering all aspects of life in the USSR. Articles and news items on the achievements of the Soviet economy; on science, technology, culture, art, and sports in the USSR; on the relationship of the Soviet Union with foreign countries; and on events abroad. Excerpts from new works of Soviet literature; words and music of popular Soviet songs; "Children's Corner." Letters to the editor. Frequent eight-page supplements consisting of documents, speeches, laws, and so on. Sample titles of recent articles: "Soviet Gymnasts Visit Japan," "XXVth Congress of the CPSU: Guaranteeing the Right to Education," "Beginning of the Tenth Five-Year Plan." 12 to 16 pages per issue. Published weekly by the Union of Soviet Societies for Friendship and Cultural Relations with Foreign Countries, 16/2 Gorky Street, Moscow, USSR. $5.50 per year. (M) Since 1930.

Narodowy Bank Polski: Information Bulletin. Detailed reports on economic conditions and developments in Poland. Coverage includes population, employment, national income, distribution of national income, foreign trade, finance, and activities of banks. "Balance-Sheet of the National Bank of Poland." Emphasis on the preceding year. About 35 pages per issue. Published yearly by the Narodowy Bank Polski (National Bank of Poland), Warsaw, Poland. Free, preferably on the basis of exchanges for foreign publications, arranged between the Economic Library of the National Bank of Poland and institutions and libraries abroad. (M)

New Albania. Pictorial magazine with primary emphasis on aspects of life in Albania. Some articles on ideology. Short stories. Letters to the editor. Sample titles of recent articles: "In the Kindergartens of the City of Elbasan," "The Museum Cities of Albania," "The Emancipation of Women as We See It." About 40 pages per issue. Published every two months by "Shqiperia e Re," Rr. Labinoti 7, Tirana, Albania. Obtainable from DREJTORIA QENDRORE E PERHAPJES DHE PROPAGANDIMIT TE LIBRIT; Bulevardi "Konferenca e Pezes," Tirana, Albania. $3.42 per year. (M) Since 1961.

New China. Pictorial magazine sympathetic to the People's Republic of China. Articles on all aspects of life in China. Book reviews; letters to the editor; "Suggested Reading." Sample titles of recent articles: "Health Care for 800 Million People," "Head Start in the Socialist Way: A Day in the Life of a Day Care Center," "Women: The Long March toward Equality." About 48 pages per issue. Published quarterly by the US-China People's Friendship Association, 41 Union Square, Room 631, New York, N. Y. 10003. $4.00 per year for individuals; $8.00 for institutions. (N/M) Since 1975.

New Hungarian Exporter. Illustrated magazine. Articles on various sectors of the Hungarian economy and on Hungarian economic development, especially as relevant to the exportation of goods and services. Sections include "Hungarian Chamber of Commerce News," "Novelties," "Science," and "Cultural Life." Some graphs and tables. Advertisements of goods Hungary offers for sale abroad. Sample titles of recent articles: "Computerized Production Control," "The Hungarian Tobacco Industry," "From Colt Farm to World Fame." 32 pages per issue. Published monthly by the Hungarian Chamber of Commerce, P.O. Box 106, H-1389 Budapest, Hungary. Obtainable from Kultura, P.O. Box 149, H-1389 Budapest 62, Hungary. $10.00 per year. (M) Since 1975.

New Hungarian Quarterly. Articles on Hungarian culture, literature, and art; on Marxist ideology as applicable to world problems; and on economic, social, and political conditions in Hungary. Short stories; poems; art reproductions. Book reviews. Section entitled "Theater and Film." Sample titles of recent articles: "The Class Content of the Policy of Detente," "City Planning in Budapest," "Thirty Years of Hungarian Architecture." 224 pages per issue. Published quarterly at 17 Rakoczi ut, 1088 Budapest, Hungary.

Obtainable from Kultura, P.O. Box 149, H-1389 Budapest 62, Hungary. $10.00 per year. (M) Since 1960.

New Polish Publications. Information on, and summaries of, Polish and foreign-language books recently published in Poland. Multipage supplement on "Soon to Appear" books. Articles relevant to book publishing in Poland. Some illustrations. Sample titles of recent articles: "Popular Scholarly Works on General History," "The Wartime Losses of Polish Culture," "Jerzy Szaniawski [Polish playwright], 1886-1970." About 28 pages per issue. Published monthly by Agpol—Foreign Trade Publicity and Publishing Enterprise, Polexportpress Division, Marazalkowska 124, 00-950 Warsaw, Poland. Obtainable from Ars Polona-Ruch, Krakowskie Przedmiescie 7, P.O. Box 1001, Warsaw, Poland. $3.85 per year. (M) Since 1952.

New Review (see New Review of East-European History).

New Review of East-European History (formerly New Review). Studies of East European affairs, with primary emphasis on historical studies. Book reviews. Published quarterly at P.O. Box 31, Postal Station E., Toronto 4, Ontario, Canada. $6.00 (Canadian) per year. (N/M) Since 1961.

New Times. Reports and commentaries on international conditions, developments, and events; on the foreign policy of the Soviet Union and of other countries; and on the activities of international organizations. Occasional supplements of documents of the Soviet government, of international organizations on foreign policy matters, and of decisions of the CPSU (Communist party of the Soviet Union) congresses and plenary meetings. A special supplement, issued once or twice a year, consists of a reference book with the declared purpose of being "of interest to those who study international affairs." Letters to the editor; questions by readers answered by the editors. Travel notes by Soviet journalists who have been a-broad. Sample titles of recent articles: "India: The People's Will," "Czechoslovakia: Rising Birth Rate," "Greece Looks to the Future." 32 pages per issue. Published weekly by "Trud," Moscow, USSR. Editorial office at Pushkin Square, Moscow 103782 GSP, USSR. Obtainable from Mezdhunarodnaya Kniga, Moscow G-200, USSR. $5.50 per year. (M) Since 1943.

New Trends in Czechoslovak Economics (see Czechoslovak Economic Digest).

New World Review. Marxist analysis of events in socialist and non-socialist countries. Publishers declare that the periodical is "de-

voted mainly to the sympathetic study of life and thought in the
USSR and the socialist world. It also concerns itself with problems
of the United Nations, former colonial countries, national liberation movements and questions of world peace and social change.
. . . It examines and furthers US-USSR cooperation and exchange
in such fields as trade, health, environment protection, science,
technology and culture. . . . [It] counters the distorted image of
the socialist world spread by the US media . . . offers its readers
factual data and thought-provoking ideas." Book reviews. Sample
titles of recent articles: "Soviet Children and the Arts," "Cuba:
Women and Child Care," "Bangladesh: The Road to Liberation."
32 pages per issue. Published monthly at 156 Fifth Avenue, Suite
308, New York, N.Y. 10010. $4.00 for one year; $7.00 for two
years; $9.50 for three years; reductions offered with purchase of
one or more books in the field: for example, a one-year subscription plus William Mandel's Soviet Women (list price, $3.50) is
offered at the regular subscription price plus $2.00. (M) Since
1932.

New Yugoslav Law. Bulletin on law and legislation in Yugoslavia.
    Published quarterly by the Union of Jurists' Association in Yugo-
    slavia, Proletariskih Brigada 24, P.O. Box 179, Belgrade, Yugo-
    slavia. $3.00 per year. (M)

News Bulletin. Bulletin of the Soviet Embassy in Canada containing
    news items on events, conditions, and developments in the Soviet
    Union and on issues relevant to Canadian-Soviet relations. Sample
    titles of recent articles: "Soviet Jews: Equals among Equals,"
    "Preparing for the 1980 Olympics" (in Moscow), "Canada's Parlia-
    mentary Delegation Visited the USSR." About five to eight pages
    per issue. Published weekly by the Press Office of the USSR Em-
    bassy in Canada, 400 Stewart Street, Apt. 1108, Ottawa, Ontario
    K1N 6L2, Canada, Free. (M)

News from Bulgaria (see Bulgarian News and Views).

News from Hungary. Reports, comments, and analyses of conditions,
    developments, and current events in Hungary. Special emphasis
    on economic and political affairs. Sample titles of recent articles:
    "New Bill Steps up Pension Rights," "Detente, Peace, and Security
    Our Aim, Says Foreign Minister," "Hungarian Team Takes World
    Title in Modern Pentathlon." About 20 pages per issue. Published
    every two months by the Press Section of the Embassy of the Hun-
    garian People's Republic, 16 Lowndes Close, London SWIX 8 BZ,
    England. Free. (M)

News from Romania. Economic, political, cultural, and other news
from Romania. Published every two weeks by the Romanian News
Agency Agerpress, Piata Scinteii 8, Bucharest, Romania. $10.00
per year. (M)

News from Ukraine. Illustrated, general-interest type newspaper.
Emphasis on Ukrainian and Soviet current events; commentaries
on important international events. Interviews with Ukrainian scientists, artists, and writers. Reprints of materials from the
Ukrainian press. Chronicle of events in the Ukrainian Republic;
section on "New Books"; letters to and from the editor. Sample
titles of recent articles: "25th Congress of Communist Party of
Soviet Union: Speech by Leonid Brezhnev," "The Soviet Way: Mas-
ters of Their Own Lives," "Air Craft Designer Oleh Antonov."
Four pages per issue. Published weekly by the Ukraine Society,
6 Zoloti Vorota Street, Kiev 252601, Ukraine, USSR. Obtainable
from Mezhdunarodnaya Kniga, Moscow G-200, USSR. $5.00 per
year. (M) Since 1964.

News of the Day. Important news events with emphasis on Romania's
relation to other countries. Sample titles of recent articles: "Ku-
wait's Parliamentary Delegation's Visit in Romania," "Meeting
between Romanian and Iraqi Trade Union Delegations," "Peoples'
Right to Self-determination Re-asserted by Romanian Representative at UN." Averages about 12 pages per issue. Published daily
by the Romanian News Agency Agerpres, Piata Scinteii 1, Bucharest, Romania. $40.00 per year. (M)

News Service. Published twice a month at Vocelova 3, Prague 2,
Czechoslovakia. (M) Since 1965. (No further information procured.)

Newsletter from behind the Iron Curtain. News reports on activities
in East Europe, with emphasis on the Baltic area. Published quarterly by the Estonian Information Centre, P.O. Box 450 30, 104
30 Stockholm C., Sweden. $2.50 per year. (N/M)

Northern Neighbors. Illustrated magazine. Emphasis on ideology,
politics, and economics. Some articles on the United States and
Canada; others on socialist countries and especially on the Soviet
Union. Described by the editors as "The Magazine of Socialism
in Action" and as "Canada's authoritative magazine reporting the
USSR." Sample titles of recent articles: "Big City Boom in Socialism [in the USSR]—And 20 New Cities Each Year," "New Year Wel-
comes Another Big Nation [Vietnam] to Socialism," "Ten Reasons
Why Capitalism Can't Make Jobs for Our Unemployed." 26 pages

per issue. Published ten times per year by Northern Neighbors
Publishing Association, Gravenhurst, Ontario POC 1GO, Canada.
$3.00 per year; $8.00 for three years. (M) Since 1951.

Obzor. Review and analysis of Bulgarian literature and the arts. Art
reproductions; short stories; poems; book reviews. Text in English and French. Sample titles of recent articles: "Writers and
the Cinema, " "A Culture which Enobles Man, " "The Last Day and
the First." About 110 pages per issue. Published quarterly by the
Committee for Friendship and Cultural Relations with Foreign
Countries of the Bulgarian Writers' Union, 39 Dondukov Boulevard,
Sofia, Bulgaria. $3.20 per year. (M) Since 1967.

OECD Economic Survey (Yugoslavia). Extensive coverage of Yugoslavia's economic performance during the year covered. Includes
information, for instance, on prices, trade, wages, indicators of
investment and consumption, industrial production, employment,
productivity, and balance of payments. Section on "Chronology of
Main Policy Measures" covering month-by-month developments.
Published for a number of OECD (Organization for Economic Cooperation and Development) member countries; but Yugoslavia is
the only socialist member country, and it has special status, participating in only some OECD activities. About 60 pages per issue.
Published annually by the Organization for Economic Cooperation
and Development, 2 rue Andre-Pascal, 75775 Paris, France. Obtainable from OECD Publications Center, 1750 Pennsylvania Avenue, N.W., Washington, D.C. 20005. $2.50. (N/M)

OECD Foreign Trade Statistics. The three series described below
cover the OECD (Organization for Economic Cooperation and Development) countries. Among the socialist countries, only Yugoslavia is a member and it has special status, participating in only
some OECD activities. However, statistics of trade of OECD countries with non-OECD countries, such as China and the USSR, are
included. Text in English and French.
Series A. Statistics of foreign trade. 112 pages per issue. Monthly. $40.00 per year by surface mail; $61.60 by airmail.

Series B. Trade by commodities—country summaries. Six volumes quarterly. Averages 135 pages per volume. $50.00 per
year by surface mail; $99.00 by airmail.

Series C. Detailed analysis by products. Imports and exports.
Several volumes per year (for instance, five volumes in 1974).
650 to 700 pages per volume. $37.50 per year by surface mail;

$74.25 by airmail. Also available separately: imports (two volumes in 1974), $17.50; exports (three volumes in 1974), $25.00.

All series are published by the Organization for Economic Cooperation and Development 2 rue Andre-Pascal, 75775 Paris, France. Obtainable from OECD Publications Center, 1750 Pennsylvania Avenue, N.W., Washington, D.C. 20005. (N/M)

Orbis. Emphasis on political and military affairs of countries around the world. Consistently carries articles on socialist countries. Book reviews. Sample titles of recent relevant articles: "The Soviet Collective Security System," "The Politics of Japan's China Decision," "The Role of Outsiders in the Cambodia Conflict." About 300 to 450 pages per issue. Published quarterly by the Foreign Policy Research Institute in association with the Fletcher School of Law and Diplomacy of Tufts University, 3508 Market St, Suite 350, Philadelphia, Pennsylvania 19104. $10.00 per year; $18.00 for two years; $25.00 for three years; student rates, $7.50, $13.00, and $18.00, respectively. (N/M) Since 1957.

Ost- Okonomi (see Economics of Planning).

Pacific Community. Main emphasis on current political and economic conditions in Asia. Many articles on nonsocialist countries, primarily Japan, but also regular contributions dealing with Asian socialist countries. Sample titles of relevant recent articles: "Sino-Soviet and Sino-Japanese Relations: A View from Jakarta," "Southeast Asia after Vietnam," "Economic Crisis and East-West Detente." Averages about 150 pages per issue. Published quarterly by the Jiji Press, Ltd., 1-3 Hibiya Park, Chiyoda-ku, Tokyo, Japan. $16.00 per year; airmail extra. (N/M) Since 1969.

Peking Informers. Emphasis on economic and political conditions and developments in China analyzed from a strongly anti-Communist point of view. One-page "Fortnightly Chronicle" reporting primarily visits of delegations and VIPs to and from China. Sample titles of recent articles: "The Epochal Significance of Liberalization of China Mainland," "Problems Posed by PRC's Founding Anniversary," "Mounting Signs of Instability and Disunity on China Mainland." Averages ten pages per issue. Published twice a month by Continental Research Institute, 199-203, Hennessy Road, 13th floor, Hong Kong. $124.00 per year. (N/M) Since 1960.

Peking Review. Chinese news about, and views on, economic, political, social, and military events with strong emphasis on international affairs. Includes speeches by high Chinese officials, important documents, articles on ideological questions, some pictures.

Most articles apparently translated from the two major Chinese newspapers, Red Flag and People's Daily. Sample titles of recent articles: "All-Round Rich Harvest in China," "Laos: Fruits of Struggle," "Soviet Union—Superpower and Superexploiter." Usually 23 pages per issue. Published weekly by Peking Review, Peking 37, China. Obtainable from Guozi Shudian, P.O. Box 399, Peking, China. $4.50 per year; $6.75 for two years; $9.00 for three years. (M) Since 1958.

People's Republic of China Press Translations. Translations from Chinese sources dealing with Chinese industry, agriculture, mining, sports, Communist party ideology, political activity, foreign affairs, the Chinese view on international events, and so on. Subscriptions include three major series: (1) a survey of newspapers covering five days of press activity; issued weekly; approximately 300 pages per issue; (2) magazine selections from nontechnical publications; issued monthly; approximately 300 pages per issue; and (3) background briefs compiled from varied sources that focus on specific topical subjects in each edition; issued irregularly; includes a quarterly index. Translations prepared by the U.S. Consulate in Hong Kong. Obtainable from U.S. Department of Commerce, National Technical Information Service (NTIS), 5285 Port Royal Road, Springfield, Virginia 22151. $275.00 per year. (M; N/M)

Persecuted Church. Religious bulletin concerned primarily with religion and the fate of the church and of believers in the Soviet Union and East Europe. Letters to the editor. Declared purpose: "To envangelize Slavic people in Communist countries and in the free world." Sample titles of recent articles: "Please Help to Save a Man," "More Soviet Oppression," "The Fate of Moseyeff Is Awaiting You." Four pages per issue. Published quarterly by The Voice of Salvation, P.O. Box 536, Montebelli, California 90640. Free. (N/M) Since 1972.

Poland. Pictorial magazine. Covers a wide variety of topics, primarily but not exclusively applicable to Poland. Primary emphasis on the arts. Section entitled "Panorama of the Month" includes latest reports on exhibitions, publications, plays, movies, and musical performances in Poland. Letters to the editor. Sample titles of recent articles: "Very Polish Plays," "Modern Medicines: Their Triumphs and Hazards," "The Prospects For Indoor Track and Field Events." 52 pages per issue. Published monthly by Koszykowa 6a, P.O. Box 310, 00-950 Warsaw, Poland. Obtainable from Ars Polona-Ruch, 7 Krakowskie Przedmiescie Street, 00-068, Warsaw, Poland. $11.00 per year. (M) Since 1954.

Poland and Germany (East and West). Economic and political conditions and developments in Poland, in the German Federal Republic (GFR), and in the German Democratic Republic (GDR). Primary focus on Polish-German historical and contemporary relations. Book reviews. Sample titles of recent articles: "Can Trade between Poland and West Germany Be Improved?," "Democratic Factor in the Re-Polonisation of Polish Western Territories," "The New Policy for Poland's Industrialization." About 50 to 65 pages per issue. Published quarterly by the Studies Centre on Polish-German Affairs, 20 Princess Gate, London SW7, England. $6.00 per year. (M; N/M). Since 1957.

Poland Tourism. Published monthly by Polska Agencja Interpress, ul. Begatela 12, 00 585 Warsaw, Poland. $4.40 per year. (M) Since 1975. (No further information procured.)

Polish Affairs. Published quarterly by the Polish Cultural Foundation, Ltd., Editorial Committee, 43 Eaton Place, SWIX 8BX London SW7, England. $3.50 per year. (U) (No further information procured.)

Polish Art Review. Pictorial magazine. Includes art reproductions; book reviews. Published quarterly by Agencja Autorska, P.O. Box 133, Dom Pod Krolami, Hipoteczna 2, Warsaw, Poland. $10.00 per year. (M) Since 1971. (No further information procured.)

Polish Co-operative Review. Pictorial magazine. Emphasis on various aspects and activities of Polish cooperatives. Sections on "Important Events" that relate to the cooperative movement (for example, "Eighth Congress of Delegates of the Union of Invalids' Cooperatives"); on "Activities of the Supreme Co-operative Council"; and on "New Co-operative Publications." Sample titles of recent articles: "Peasant Self-Aid: Cooperatives Provide Complex Self Services for Farmers," "Improvements of Social and Educational Activity in Co-operative Settlements," "Christmas Trees Produced by Co-operatives." 40 pages per issue. Published quarterly by the Supreme Co-operative Council, ul. Jasna 1, pok. 413, Warsaw, Poland. Free. (M) Since 1967.

Polish Economic Survey. Focus on Poland's economy and economic relations with foreign countries. Sample titles of recent articles: "Exploring Natural Resources of Poland," "Development Trends in Motorization," "Sweden: Development of Trade Regulations." About 15 pages per issue. Published twice a week by Agpol, Marszalkowska 124, P.O. Box 726, 00-068 Warsaw, Poland. Obtainable from Ars Polona-Ruch, Krakowskie Przedmiescie 7,

P.O. Box 1001, Warsaw, Poland. $15.00 per year by air. (M)
Since 1961.

Polish Facts and Figures. Illustrated periodical. Focus on political,
economic, social, and cultural events, conditions, and developments in Poland. Special emphasis on Poland's relations with Britain. Sample titles of recent articles: "Warsaw: A City of Light,
Charm, and Elegance," "Main Prerequisites for the Further Development of Economic Co-operation between Poland and the United
Kingdom," "Agreement on Scientific Co-operation between the
Polish Academy of Sciences and the Royal Society." Eight to ten
pages per issue. Published irregularly, one or two times per year,
by the Press Office of the Polish Embassy, 47 Portland Place,
WIN 3AG, London W1, England. Free (M) Since 1946.

Polish Fair Magazine. Illustrated magazine. Focus on Poland's foreign trade, on commodities and groups of commodities Poland exports, on the Poznan International Fairs (several each year), and
on Poland's participation in fairs in other countries. Extensive
advertisements of products Poland offers for sale abroad. Sample
titles of recent articles: "UNIVERSAL: Exporter of Goods Well-
Known All over the World," "Economic Exhibition 'Poland - 75' in
Brussels," "Poland and Development of Socialist Economic Integration of the CMEA Countries." About 50 pages per issue. Published quarterly by Agpol—Foreign Trade Publicity and Publishing
Enterprise, Polexportpress Division, Marszalkowska 124, P.O.
Box 726, Warsaw, Poland. Obtainable from Ars Polona-Ruch,
Krakowskie Przedmiescie 7, P.O. Box 1001, Warsaw, Poland.
$4.80 per year; a limited number of copies have been designated
by Agpol (see address above) for distribution free of charge on request; but systematic receipt of successive issues can be guaranteed
only to paid-up subscribers. (M)

Polish Film/Film Polonais. Text in English and French. Published
every two months by Film Polski-Export and Import of Films, ul.
Mazowiecka 6/8, 00048 Warsaw, Poland. $4.80 per year. (M)
Since 1963. (No further information procured.)

Polish Foreign Trade. Illustrated magazine. Focus on Poland's international economic relations. Advertisements of products Poland offers for sale abroad or wishes to import. Occasional reviews of relevant books. Sample titles of recent articles: "Towards
Normalization of East-West Trade," "How to Operate on the Polish
Market," "Polish Affairs in Sweden." About 40 pages per issue.
Published monthly by Agpol—Foreign Trade Publicity and Publishing Enterprise, Polexportpress Division, Marszalkowska 124,

00-950 Warsaw, Poland. Obtainable from Ars Polona-Ruch, Krakowskie Przedmiescie 7, P.O. Box 1001, Warsaw, Poland. $8.80 per year. (M) Since 1954.

Polish Literature/Littérature Polonaise. Articles on contemporary Polish literature. Text in English and French. Book reviews. Published quarterly by Agencija Autorska, Box 113, Dom Pod Krolami, Hipoteczka, Warsaw, Poland. $8.00 per year. (M) Since 1968.

Polish Maritime News. Pictorial magazine. Information on shipping, shipbuilding, harbors, fishing, and related subjects. Sections on "Maritime Law," "CMEA News," and "Books Received." Special section with statistical information in every third issue. Sample titles of recent articles: "Poland's Position in World Shipbuilding," "Polish Coal in World Seaborne Trade," "Polish Exports of Fish and Fish Products." 20 pages per issue. Published monthly (except for a combined July-August issue, which has 40 pages) by the Polish Chamber of Foreign Trade, Maritime Branch, ul. Pulaskiego 6, 81-963 Gdynia, Poland. Obtainable from Ars-Polona Ruch, Krakowskie Przedmiescie 7, Warsaw, Poland. $9.00 per year. (M) Since 1958.

Polish Music/Polnische Musik. Illustrated booklet. Emphasis on contemporary, and especially Polish, music. Section on "New Polish Compositions"; "Music Chronicle" with day-by-day accounts of performances by Polish musicians abroad, concerts at which Polish compositions were played, and so on. Side-by-side English and German text. Sample titles of recent articles: "3rd Warsaw Composers Concert in Leningrad," "The New Music Museum in Poland," "Polish Music in Britain." 48 pages per issue. Published quarterly by Agencja Autorska, Hipoteczna 2, Warsaw, Poland. $8.00 per year. (M) Since 1966.

Polish News Bulletin of the American and British Embassies. Translations of articles, passages, and commentary from the daily and weekly press of Poland and from a variety of Polish monthlies and other, special-interest publications. Primary emphasis on politics and economics with occasional items in other areas, such as culture or science. Frequent "annexes" containing texts of important speeches, communiqués, international agreements, and so on. Sample titles of recent articles: "XV Session of the Polish-Yugoslav Economic Cooperation Committee," "Gradual Increase in Milk Supplies," "Preparations for Conference of European Communist and Workers' Parties." About 20 to 30 pages per issue. Published daily by the U.S. and British embassies in Warsaw. Obtainable from the Embassy of the United States of America, Warsaw, Poland. $300.00 per year. (M)

Polish Perspectives. Essays on recent history and present life in Poland with special emphasis on economic and political affairs. Sections entitled "Press in Review," "Economy and Life," "Arts and Science." Book reviews. Sample titles of recent articles: "Consumption Model for Tomorrow," "The Warsaw Treaty 1955-75," "The Polish Way of Sex." About 105 pages per issue. Published monthly under the auspices of the Polish Institute of International Affairs, P.O. Box 159, Warecka 1A, 00-950 Warsaw, Poland. Obtainable from Ruch, P.O. Box 154, Warsaw, Poland. $9.90 per year. (M) Since 1958.

Polish Review. Primarily articles on Polish history. Frequently contains symposiums, selected proceedings of relevant conferences, and so on. Book reviews. Sample titles of recent articles: "Soviet Policy toward Poland, 1926-29," "Tolerance and Intolerance in Poland: The Two Political Traditions." About 150 pages per issue. Published quarterly by the Polish Institute of Arts and Sciences in America, 59 East 66th Street, New York, N.Y. 10021. $10.00 per year. (N/M) Since 1956.

Polish Sociological Bulletin. Articles on sociology and on sociological problems, with primary emphasis on subjects relevant to Poland. Reports on international sociological conferences in which Poland participates. Book reviews. Sample titles of recent articles: "The Practical Application of Industrial Sociology in Poland," "The Process of Reintegration in Post-War Communities in Poland," "Cultural Determination of Attitudes." About 60 to 85 pages per issue. Published twice a year by the Polish Sociological Association, Nowy Swiat 72, 00-330 Warsaw, Poland. Obtainable from Ruch, P.O. Box 154, Warsaw, Poland. $3.00 per year. (M) Since 1961.

Polish Weekly. Current events, with emphasis on economics, politics, and culture. Speeches by government and Party officials. Survey of the Polish press; "Topics of the Week," consisting of short, primarily political items; "New Books," listed and briefly described. One short story in each issue. Sample titles of recent articles: "The Constitution of Socialist Poland," "A Secondary Education for All," "Jubilee Year of the National Philharmonic Orchestra." Published weekly by the Polish Press Agency, Al. Jerozolimskie 7, 00-950 Warsaw, Poland. $19.00 per year by air. (M)

Polish Western Affairs. Focus on present-day economic, political, and social problems of Germany and Central Europe, on conditions and progress in Poland, and on other news items of interest to

Poles residing in Germany. Book reviews. Sample titles of recent articles: "Poland, the German Problem and the Two German States (1944-1974)," "State and Society—The Building of Socialism in People's Poland," "The Evolution of the Socio-professional Status of the Intelligentsia in People's Poland." About 150 pages per issue. Published twice a year by Instytut Zechodni (Institute for Western Affairs), Star Rynek 78/79, Poznan, Poland. Obtainable from Ruch, Wilcza 46, Warsaw, Poland. $2.00 per year. (M) Since 1960.

Polish Western Association of America: Quarterly (see Quarterly of the Polish Western Association of America).

Political Affairs. Official organ of the Communist party of the United States. Emphasis on Marxist ideology and on analyses of political and economic events, conditions, and developments, primarily in the United States but also elsewhere. Book reviews. Declares itself the "Theoretical Journal of the Communist Party, U.S.A." Sample titles of recent articles: "On the Materiality of Mind," "U.S. Imperialism and the Intelligence Agencies," "Senile Capitalism, Racism and Slavery." 64 pages per issue. Published monthly by Political Affairs Publishers, 23 West 26th Street, New York, N.Y. 10010. $7.50 per year. (M) Since 1922.

Press Review. Translations and summaries of news items in all fields from major Czechoslovak newspapers, primarily from Rude Pravo. Regular sections entitled "Summary of the Main News Coverage and Comment," "News in Detail," and "News in Brief." Sample titles of recent articles, translated in full or summarized: "House of the People Debates the Power Situation," "Espionage against Czechoslovakia from the Austrian Territory," "Party Central Control and Auditing Commission Meets." About six pages per issue. Published five times per week by the Press Section of the British Embassy in Prague, Czechoslovakia. Obtainable from Publications Procurement Office, American Embassy, Prague, c/o Department of State, Washington, D.C. 20521. $188.00 per year for single subscriptions, mailed once a week; $20.00 for each additional subscription mailed to the same subscriber. (M)

Press Summary. Translations of items carried in Hungarian national daily newspapers. Emphasis on internal developments, international events involving Hungary, and the development of communism. Translations of announcements, speeches, documents, and so on. Most translations verbatim; items deemed of lesser interest sometimes summarized. Occasional supplements consisting of translations of items deemed of special importance and interest from the main monthly periodicals—Partelet and Tarsadalmi Szemle (the Hungarian Socialist Workers' party's periodicals). Sample titles of recent press translations: "Communique on the Session of the Central Committee of the Hungarian Socialist Workers' Party," "Hungarian-Yugoslav Cooperation in Standardization," "Jasser Arafat Received by Janos Kadar." 4 to 20 pages per issue. Published six days per week by the British Embassy, Budapest, Hungary. 500 forints per month; progressive discounts for larger orders; 20 forints per month for ten or more subscriptions. (M)

Problems of Communism. Articles on all aspects of communism; events, conditions, and developments in socialist countries; activities of Communist parties in nonsocialist countries; and related topics. Contributors include professors, journalists, political analysts from Radio Free Europe and Radio Liberty, and free-lance writers, and their articles "do not necessarily reflect the views or policies of the United States government." Book reviews; book review articles; letters to the editor published in a section entitled "Notes and Views." Declared purpose: "to provide analyses and significant background information on various aspects of world communism today." Sample titles of recent articles: "Soviet Strategy in the Balkans," "The Shifting Sands of Arab Communism," "North Vietnam since Ho." 80 to 90 pages per issue. Published every two months by the U.S. Information Agency, 1776 Pennsylvania Avenue, N.W., Washington, D.C. 20547. Within the United States, obtainable from Superintendent of Documents, U.S. Government Printing Office, Washington, D.C. 20547. $9.35 per year. Obtainable outside of the United States "in most cases" free of charge by writing to the nearest office of the U.S. Information Agency; also obtainable from the U.S. Government Printing Office for foreign mailing at $11.75 per year. 25 percent discount for orders of 100 or more mailed to a single address. (N/M) Since 1974.

Problems of Economics. Unabridged translations of articles on economic theory, practice, and policy, drawn from the whole range of Soviet economic scholarship. Sample titles of recent articles: "Problems of Long-Range Planning and Forecasting," "The Economics of Natural Resources," "Is Galbraith Crossing the Rubicon?" Averages 85 to 90 pages per issue. Published monthly by the International Arts and Sciences Press, 901 North Broadway, White Plains, New York 10603. $100.00 per year for institutions; $30.00 for individuals associated with subscribing institutions. (M) Since 1958.

Problems of Peace and Socialism (see World Marxist Review).

Problems of the Contemporary World. Interdisciplinary Soviet journal. Articles in many social science disciplines, with emphasis
on the USSR and on matters of special interest to the USSR. Sample titles of recent articles: "Social and Economic Aspects of China's Population Problem," "NEP: A Policy of Transition to Socialism," "National Relations in the USSR: Theory and Practice."
About 140 pages per issue. Published by Social Sciences Today,
33/12 Arbat, Moscow 121002, USSR. Obtainable from Mezhdunarodnaya Kniga, Moscow G-200, USSR. Price and frequency of
publication not given. (M)

Problems of the Far East. Soviet description and analysis of contemporary social, political, and economic problems; problems of
ideology; culture and language; foreign policy; international relations of the countries and peoples of the Far East and Southeast
Asia. Published quarterly in Moscow. Obtainable from Mezhdun-
arondaya Kniga, Moscow G-200, USSR. $6.00 per year. (M)

Pyongyang Times. Newspaper concerned primarily with political,
economic, social, and cultural development in North Korea, with
comparisons between North and South Korea and with related topics. Sample titles of recent articles: "Power Production Increase
through Intensified Technical Innovation Movement," "Two Dia-
metrically Different Realities: North and South of Korea as Seen
from Public Health Services" "US Must Pull Its Armed Forces
Back From S. Korea Immediately in Accordance with UN Resolution." Four pages per issue. Published weekly by Pyongyang
Times, Pyongyang, Democratic People's Republic of Korea. 10
chon per issue. (M)

Quarterly Economic Review. Seventy-seven such reviews are published, five of them dealing with oil in various parts of the world.
The others each deal with an individual country or with a number
of countries; eight of these cover exclusively, or include in their
coverage, socialist countries:

Serial number	Title
15	China, Hong Kong, North Korea
17	Cuba, Dominican Republic, Haiti, Puerto Rico
51	Czechoslovakia, Hungary
66	Indochina: Vietnam, Laos, Cambodia
19	Poland, East Germany
63	Romania, Bulgaria, Albania
48	USSR
50	Yugoslavia

Each Quarterly Economic Review (except the five specifically devoted to oil) contains a 300-word summary of its contents; a brief
short-term forecast of main trends in the economy; 500 to 1,000
words of news analysis covering political developments relevant
to an understanding of the economy, government economic policies,
trends in investment and consumer spending, and performance of
key business indicators; an evaluation of foreign trade data; and
an assessment of development plans. Charts of the main economic
trends; statistical appendixes. Subscribers also receive an annual
reference supplement that contains background data on political
and economic developments and on key long-run trends. Each
Quarterly Economic Review is published quarterly by The Economist Intelligence Unit, Spencer House, 27 St. James Place, London SW1A 1NT, England. $53.00 per Review per year; progressive
discounts for more than four Reviews (five for $262.00 per year;
six for $312.00; seven and eight for $362.00, $412.00). Duplicate
subscriptions (one only for each Review taken), $21.00 per year.
Airmail outside Europe, add $5.00 for each Review. (N/M)
1952.

Quarterly of the Polish Western Association of America. Devoted primarily to questions of Polish-German relations. Section entitled
"German Chronicle" dealing with current political events in Germany, with such articles as "Bonn-Prague Treaty" and "Government's Trouble." Occasional book reviews. Sample titles of recent articles: "Polish-West German Discussion on Textbooks,"
"The Treaty Between Poland and the G.F.R., and the Charter of
the United Nations," "Confession of an Admirer of Germany." 16
to 20 pages per issue. Published three times a year by the Polish
Western Association, 1130 North Ashland, Chicago, Illinois 60622.
Free, but donations to the Quarterly are invited. (N/M)

Radio Free Europe Research Publications on East European Affairs.
Papers on the most important aspects of the internal situations in
the five countries to which Radio Free Europe (RFE) broadcasts
(Bulgaria, Czechoslovakia, Hungary, Poland, and Romania); on
their relations with the Soviet Union and with each other; on Comecon and Warsaw Pact developments; on the Yugoslav situation; on
developments in Communist movements elsewhere in the world; on
East-West relations; and on related subjects. Subscription includes
four series:

1. Situation Report. Each deals with a specific subject. Sample
titles of recently published items: Czechoslovakia: Wholesale Price
Reform Delayed, Hungary: Bottlenecks in the Educational System,

Poland: Reshuffle in the Ministries Continues. Two to three pages per item. Usually published weekly, about two to eight items per week (for instance, during fiscal year 1974/75, 921 Situation Report items were published).

2. Background Report. Usually deals with themes of broader significance. Sample titles of recent articles: "Polish Trade and Polish Trends: Economic and Political Consideration," "Icy Winds over the Bulgarian Literary Landscape," "Changes in Albanian Leadership Signify Struggle for Succession to Power." Averages eight to nine pages per report. Published irregularly, about four per week (during fiscal year 1974/75, 208 Background Reports were published).

3. Press Survey. Translations of important articles from the press of the five countries to which RFE broadcasts, with emphasis on economic and political conditions and developments. Sample titles of recent articles: Hungarian Press Survey: "Is the Development of the Market an Objective Law of Socialism?" Czechoslovak Press Survey: "The Principles of Responsibility in Joint Planning." Rumanian Press Survey: "Equalizing the Levels of Economic Planning—An International Duty of Socialist Countries." Averages about eight to nine pages per issue. Published irregularly, several per month; over half of them on Czechoslovakia.

4. Communist Party-Government Line-up. Up-to-date lists of names and titles of officeholders in the Communist parties and governments of Albania, Bulgaria, Czechoslovakia, the GDR, Hungary, Poland, Romania, the USSR, and Yugoslavia. Published rarely, but revised pages are issued as changes occur. About 32 pages.

Radio Free Europe Research Publications on East European Affairs are published by Information Services, Radio Free Europe/Radio Liberty, 1 Englischer Garten, 8000 Munich 22, Germany. Obtainable from Radio Free Europe/Radio Liberty, 1201 Connecticut Avenue, N.W., Washington, D.C. 20036. $50.00 per year. Joint subscription with Radio Liberty Research Publications on Soviet Affairs (see below), $75.00 per year. (M; N/M)

Radio Liberty Research Publications on Soviet Affairs. Research reports on the most important aspects of the internal situation in the Soviet Union, on the USSR's relationship with other countries, and on related topics. About 400 formal research reports per year. Of the 440 such reports issued in 1974, for instance, 139 were devoted to economic themes, 87 to culture and literature, 86 to political issues, 43 to foreign affairs, 40 to military matters, 22 to nationalities, and 23 to miscellaneous topics. Subscriptions include six series:

1. Radio Liberty Research (formerly Radio Liberty Dispatch). Analyses of current conditions, developments, and events. Each issue devoted to one topic. Sample titles of recent issues: Fifteen Years of Soviet-Albanian Impasse and No Breakthrough in Sight, Highlights of 1975 in Foreign Affairs, Stalin's Ghost Resurrected as CPSU Congress Approaches. From one to twenty pages per issue. Published irregularly, several times per week.

2. Radio Liberty Research Supplements. Studies and analyses more extensive than those published in Radio Liberty Research. Each issue devoted to one topic. Usually in English; occasionally in Russian. Sample titles of recent issues: Soviet Economic Growth: Past, Present and Projected, A Survey of Soviet Agriculture in 1974, Soviet Literary Criminals. Averages about 20 pages per supplement. Published irregularly, about six to ten times per year.

3. Current Abstracts. Summaries of recent articles and publications on Soviet affairs, prepared with the aid of staff members from all divisions of Radio Liberty. Some articles from Western media and from emigré publications. Some parts in Russian, others in English. Sample titles of recent articles: "History of USSR Academy of Sciences," "Latvia: Komsomol and Country Schools," "A Sympathetic Critique of Camus." Averages about 15 to 20 pages per issue. Published twice a month.

4. Soviet Media Review. Translations, summaries, and comments on items from the Soviet press. Two to six pages per issue. Published irregularly, about once a week.

5. Chronology of Soviet Affairs. Emphasis on political and economic events. Published every seven months. About 280 pages per issue.

6. Miscellaneous items. Samizdat (underground) indexes, translations of Radio Liberty broadcasts, calendar of forthcoming events and anniversaries, and other ad hoc publications. Published irregularly.

Radio Liberty Research Publications on Soviet Affairs are published by Information Services, Radio Free Europe/Radio Liberty, 1 Englischer Garten, 8000 Munich 22, Germany. Obtainable from Radio Free Europe/Radio Liberty, 1201 Connecticut Ave., N.W., Washington, D.C. 20036. $50.00 per year. Joint subscription with Radio Free Europe Research Publications on East European Affairs (see above), $75.00 per year. (M; N/M)

RCDA—Religion in Communist Dominated Areas. Excerpts of articles on religion, translated primarily from the press of socialist countries; some translations from religious underground publications and from the press of nonsocialist countries. Translations are accompanied by introductions, commentaries, and analyses. Some cartoons. Declared purpose: "to make available and to analyze information on the attitudes and practices of Communist Parties with respect to the life, work and vital concerns of believers in Communist countries. Particular attention is given to the violation of religious freedom and other human rights in all closed societies." Sample titles of recent articles: "Religious Persecution in Lithuania," "Hungarian Christianity Has Found Its Place in the Socialist Society," "Solzhenitsyn Warns Against False Detente." Temporarily published quarterly instead of bimonthly or monthly, with 48 instead of some 30 pages per issue, by the Research Center for Religious and Human Rights in Closed Societies, Ltd., 475 Riverside Drive, New York, N.Y. 10027. $15.00 per year. (M; N/M) Since 1962.

Religion in Communist Dominated Areas (see RCDA—Religion in Communist Dominated Areas).

Religion in Communist Lands. Emphasis on religion in socialist countries and on related subjects. Book reviews, documents, letters to the editor, extensive section on "News in Brief," extensive bibliography of (a) samizdat (underground, self-published material) from or about religious groups in the USSR and (b) significant Soviet press articles on religion and atheism. Sample titles of recent articles: "Church-State Relations in Yugoslavia Since 1967," "Monasticism in the Soviet Union," "Early Twentieth Century Russia: Church and State." About 72 pages per issue. Published quarterly by the Centre for the Study of Religion and Communism, Keston College, Heathfield Road, Keston, Kent BR2 6BA, England. $10.00 per year; $12.50 by airmail. (N/M)

Reprints from the Soviet Press. Selected articles, speeches, documents, and reports translated from the Soviet press. Emphasis on world economic and political news items and analyses. Sample titles of recent articles: "USSR-West Europe, Scientific and Technical Cooperation," "The Pentagon's 'Post-Vietnam' Stakes," "India: Along the Road to Progress." About 54 to 78 pages per issue. Published every two weeks by Compass Publications, 101 Old Mamaroneck Road, Box No. 3B-6, White Plains, New York 10605. $35.00 per year. (M) Since 1965.

Review (Belgrade). Pictorial magazine. Articles on various aspects of life in Yugoslavia. Emphasis on culture and tourist attractions. Letters to the editor. Some advertisements of products Yugoslavia offers for sale abroad. Sample titles of recent articles: "Zagreb—

The Most Cosmopolitan Cuisine in Europe," "Modern Art Trea-
sures in Skopje," "Non-alignment: A Worldwide Platform." 46
pages per issue. Published 11 times per year by Tourist Press,
Terazije 31, Belgrade, Yugoslavia. 60 dinars per year. (M)
Since 1963.

Review (London). Emphasis on political, social, and economic conditions and developments in Yugoslavia, analyzed by native Yugo-
slavians residing in the West and occasionally by other Western
researchers critical of the present regime in Yugoslavia. Bibliography; chronicle of events. Sample titles of recent articles:
" 'Tito, We Love Thee'—The Personality Cult in Self-management
Socialism," "Nationality and the National Question," "The History
behind Yugoslavia's Psychological Deterrent." Averages about 90
pages per issue. Published irregularly, approximately once a
year, by the Study Center for Yugoslav Affairs, 62 Offley Road
London, SW9, England. $3.00 per issue. (N/M) Since 1960.

Review (Tokyo). English translations of articles originally published
in Japanese, taken primarily from Kyosanken Mondai (Communist
Bloc Problems). Focus on communism, on the socialist countries
(especially the Soviet Union and China), and on the relations of socialist and nonsocialist countries. Sample titles of recent articles:
"New Perspectives for Chinese Communism—Cultural Revolution
and After," "The Soviet Union and Africa," "New Stage of Sino-
Japanese Relationship and International Relations in Asia." 26 to
97 pages per issue. Published quarterly by the Communist Affairs
Division, Japan Institute of International Affairs, Mori Building
No. 19, 40-2 Shiba Kotohiracho, Minato-ku, Tokyo, 105 Japan.
$6.00 per year. (N/M)

Review of International Affairs. Covers a wide range of topics with
emphasis on international politics, economics, law, science, and
culture, especially as related to Yugoslavia. Speeches; documents.
Sample titles of articles: "Africa and Socialism," "Dimensions of
the Vietnamese Victory," "The Present Moment in Yugoslav Literature." 30 to 36 pages per issue. Published twice a month by
Medunarodna Politika, P.O. Box 413, Nemanjina 34, 11000 Belgrade, Yugoslavia. $6.00 per year. (M) Since 1950.

Review of Socialist Law. Articles on various aspects of legality and
law in socialist countries. Translations of Soviet and East European laws. Book reviews. Declared purpose: "The scholarly study
of socialist law and the dissemination of legal information on the
basis of such study. . . . The Review is intended to provide up-
to-date information on new legal developments and general access

to legal materials which would otherwise be difficult to locate."
Sample titles of recent articles: "Soviet Penitentiary Law," "Equity
and Its Social Equivalent in the Polish Legal System," "Comparing
Chinese Enterprise Administration and Settlement of Contract Dis-
putes with Soviet Practices." About 75 to 100 pages per issue.
Published quarterly by A. W. Sijthoff International Publishing Com-
pany BV in cooperation with the Documentation Office for East
European Law of the University of Leyden, Rapenburg 82, Leyden,
The Netherlands. $30.50 per year. (M; N/M) Since 1975.

RMASS Newsletter. Primarily announcements of and reports on conferences, messages from the RMASS (Rocky Mountain Association
for Slavic Studies) president, and other relevant information items
(such as news that the newly established Institute for Advanced
Russian Studies in Washington, D.C., will prepare a published in-
ventory of archival materials in the United States pertaining to
Russia). The RMASS intends to "gradually expand the Newsletter
to include notes, queries, commentaries, discussions, and sugges-
tions reflecting a growing intellectual activity among scholars in
the area." Published three times a year (January, April, October)
by the RMASS. Obtainable from Libor Brom, University of Denver,
Denver, Colorado 80202. Free to RMASS members; membership
dues: $2.00 per year for regular memberships; $3.00 for husband-
wife memberships. (N/M)

Rocky Mountain Association for Slavic Studies Newsletter (see RMASS
Newsletter).

Romania: Articles, Features, Information. Articles, feature reports,
and information on a wide range of subjects reflective of Romania's
domestic and foreign policy. Sample titles of recent articles: "Romania's Activity in the United Nations," "Achievements and Trends
in Romanian Education," "Ample Investment Programme under
1976-1980 Five-Year Plan." Averages about 18 pages per issue.
Since September 1975 it has frequently included a multipage supplement entitled Romanian Viewpoints (see below). Published monthly
by the Romanian News Agency Agerpres, Piata Scinteii 1, Bucharest, Romania. $15.00 per year. (M) Since 1973.

Romania: Documents-Events. Important speeches, documents re-
leased by the Romanian government or by the Communist party of
Romania, reports on meetings and conferences in which the Romanian government or Communist party are represented, and so
on. Sample titles of recent articles: "Meeting of Executive Committee of CC of RCP [Central Committee of the Romanian Communist Party]," "Communique on the Visit of Romanian Prime Minis-

ter Manea Manescu to the Socialist Federal Republic of Yugoslavia, "
"Official Visit to Romania by British Premier Harold Wilson: Joint
Communique." Averages about 40 pages per issue. Published
weekly by the Romanian News Agency Agerpres, Piata Scinteii 1,
Bucharest, Romania. $20.00 per year. (M) Since 1973.

Romania Today. Illustrated magazine. Emphasis on aspects of life
in Romania. Advertisements of products Romania offers for sale
abroad. Sample titles of recent articles: "Romania and the Major
Economic Issues of Our Days, " "The Law of Force must be Replaced by the Force of Law, " "The Family Today." About 67 pages
per issue. Published monthly at Piata Scinteii 1, Corp. B I,
Oficiul Postal 33, Bucharest, Romania. Obtainable from Ilexim,
Press Export-Import Department, Calea Grivitei 64-68, P.O.
Box 2001, Bucharest, Romania. $5.00 per year. (M) Since 1955.

Romanian Books. Illustrated bulletin, tabloid format. Articles on
Romanian books, book publishing, and related topics. Descriptions
of new books; Writers' Union awards; section on "Romanian Writers
of Today"; bibliography of books published during preceding six
months. Sample titles of recent articles: "Prizes Awarded to Romanian Books [at an international exhibition], " "Culture and Civilization: The Romanian Book between 1918-1948, " "Listening to the
Voices of the Old Chroniclers." 64 pages per issue. Published
quarterly by Publishing Centre, Foreign Relations Department 1,
Piata Scinteii, Bucharest, Romania. Obtainable from I.C.E.
Ilexim, Book Export-Import Department, Calea Grivitei 64-66,
Bucharest 7000, Romania. $5.00 per year. (M) Since 1964.

Romanian Bulletin. Articles on all aspects of life in Romania and on
topics of interest to residents of the United States concerned with
Romania. Declared purpose: "to make better known throughout the
United States of America various aspects of contemporary Romanian society, mainly political, social, economic, scientific, cultural and artistic life, as well as significant moments in the cultural history of the people and in Romanian-American relations. "
Poems by Romanian poets; book reviews. Sample titles of recent
articles: "Romania and Non-alignment, " "The Status of Women in
Romania, " "Alba Iulia: A Two Millenium-Old Town." Usually
eight, but sometimes four, pages per issue. Published monthly by
the Romanian Library, 866 Second Avenue, New York, N.Y. 10017.
Free. (M) Since 1964.

Romanian Film (see Film Roumain/Romanian Film).

Romanian Foreign Trade. Pictorial magazine. Focus on aspects of
the Romanian economy that affect Romania's international economic

relations and especially its exports. Sections on the Romanian economy, on the country's economic and commercial relations with
other countries, on fairs and exhibitions, on relevant laws, and
on tourism. Section entitled "The Exporters' Offer" dealing with
specific products or groups of products Romania offers for sale
abroad. Advertisements of such products or group of products.
Sample titles of recent articles: "The Romanian Textile Industry,"
"Constanta: Romania's Gate to the Sea," "Prospects for the Further
Extension of Foreign Trade." 48 to 64 pages per issue. Published
quarterly by PUBLICOM, Foreign Trade Publicity Agency, N.
Balcescu Boulevard, Bucharest 22, Romania. $15.00 per year.
(M) Since 1950.

Romanian Review. Illustrated magazine. Focus on literature, art,
and the performing arts in Romania. Essays; poems; theater reviews; film reviews; book reviews; music. Sample titles of recent
articles: "Some Notes on the Female (the Virile) Spirit in Romanian Art," "The World Drama on the Romanian Stages," "American
Literature Viewed by Romanian Critics." About 150 to 160 pages
per issue. Published quarterly at Piata Scinteii 1, Bucharest, Romania. Obtainable from Ilexim, P.O. Box 2001, Bucharest, Romania. $5.00 per year. (M) Since 1946.

Romanian Scientific Abstracts: Social Sciences. English-language abstracts of articles originally published in Romanian journals.
Fields covered are economics, philosophy, logic, sociology, psychology, history, archeology, ethnography, literature and the arts,
jurisprudence, linguistics, and philology. Sample titles of recent
articles: "The Notion of Materialism in Lenin's View," "A Few
Considerations on National Income Redistribution," "On the Formation of the Romanian Nation." Published every two months by
the Socialist Republic of Romania, Scientific Documentation Service, str. Gutenberg, nr. 3 Bis., Bucharest 6, Romania. Obtainable from Rompresfilatelia, Cal. Grivitei 64-66, Box 2001, Bucharest, Romania. 240 lei per year. (M) Since 1964.

Romanian Sources. Articles by Western contributors and translations
of Romanian texts in the fields of Romanian history, philosophy,
economics, literature, literary criticism, folklore, and others of
interest to students of Romanian culture and civilization. Occasional poems. Book reviews. Sample titles of recent articles: "The
Psychology of the Romanian People," "Romania under Alexandru
Ioan Cuza," "Romanian Collection at the University of Pittsburgh:
An Annotated Bibliography." 65 to 85 pages per issue. Published
twice a year by the University of Pittsburgh Libraries and the
American Romanian Institute for Research, G 27 Hillman Library,

University of Pittsburgh, Pittsburgh, Pennsylvania 15260. $5.00
per year; $3.00 for students. (M; N/M) Since 1975.

Romanian Viewpoints. Translations of major articles from the Romanian press and especially from Romania's leading daily, Scin-
teia, focusing primarily on international politics. Sample titles of
recent articles: "A Major Conclusion of Recent Special Session of
[U.N.] General Assembly," "Expression of Socialist Romania's
Solidarity with Developing Countries in the Fight for the Building
of a New World Economic and Political Order," "For a Political
Settlement of the Conflictual [sic] Situation, for a Just and Lasting
Peace in the Middle East." Varying lengths (recent issues from
10 to 18 pages). Published several times per year as a supplement
to Romania: Articles, Features, Information (see above) by the
Romanian News Agency Agerpres, Piata Scinteii 1, Bucharest,
Romania. Free to subscribers of Romania: Articles, Features,
Information. (M)

Russian History. Devoted exclusively to Russian history (medieval,
imperial, and Soviet). Contributions include papers on cultural
and intellectual history. Occasional notes, translations, documents.
Book reviews; professional news. Sample titles of recent articles:
"Industrialization, Factory Life and Social Stability: Moscow and
the Central Industrial Region, 1870-1900," "The Moscow Bourgeoi-
sie and Tsarism during World War I (1914-1917)," "Entering the
Comintern: Negotiations between the Bolsheviks and Western So-
cialists at the Second Congress of the Communist International,
1920." About 100 to 125 pages per issue. Published twice a year
(quarterly publication planned for the future) by the University
Center for International Studies (UCIS), University of Pittsburgh,
218 Oakland Avenue, Pittsburgh, Pennsylvania 15260. Obtainable
from UCIS Publications Section, University Center of International
Studies, C-6 Mervis Hall, University of Pittsburgh, Pittsburgh,
Pennsylvania 15260. $15.00 per year for institutions; $12.50 for
faculty; $8.00 for full-time students; lower prices to subscribers
taking more than one UCIS journal. For more specific information
on discounts, see UCIS Journals. (N/M) Since 1974.

Russian Review. Articles on Russian history, politics, social and
economic institutions and developments, culture, art, literature,
and so on. Declared purpose: "to interpret the real aims and aspirations of the Russian people, as distinguished from and con-
trasted with Soviet Communism, and to advance general knowledge
of Russian culture, history, and civilization." Documents; book
notices; book reviews; review articles. Sample titles of recent
articles: "Catherine the Great and the Problem of Female Rule,"

"The Samizdat [underground publishing] Movement in the USSR,"
"Soviet-American Relations: Hopes and Anxiety." About 100 to
125 pages per issue. Published quarterly by The Russian Review,
The Hoover Institution on War, Revolution, and Peace, Stanford,
California 94305. $12.00 per year; $8.00 for students. (N/M)
Since 1941.

SBCS. Statni Banka Ceskoslovenska: Bulletin (see Statni Banka
Ceskoslovenska: Bulletin).

Science and Society. Research articles, primarily on ideological,
philosophical, and historical topics, presented from a Marxist
point of view. Book reviews. Declares itself to be "An Independent
Journal of Marxism." Sample titles of recent articles: "Notes on
the Historical Application of Marxist Cultural Theory," "Contro-
versies in the Theory of Surplus Value: Old and New," "European
Feudalism and Middle Eastern Despotism." About 125 pages per
issue. Published quarterly at 445 West 59th Street, New York,
N.Y. 10019. $8.00 per year. (M) Since 1936.

Selected Trade and Economic Data of the Centrally Planned Economies.
Tables, charts, and graphs containing economic data on 15 indus-
trialized nonsocialist and eight socialist countries, the latter being
the USSR, China, Bulgaria, Czechoslovakia, the GDR, Hungary,
Poland, and Romania. Emphasis on production and trade data.
Sample titles of tables, charts, and graphs: "Bulgaria: Estimated
Gross National Product at Market Prices (1965-73)," "East Ger-
man Trade with the U.S., 1965-1974," "Trade Shares Data, USSR,
1965-73: USSR Exports and Imports from Selected Trading Groups."
About 65 pages per issue. Published yearly by the Bureau of East-
West Trade U.S. Department of Commerce, Room 4813, 14th
Street and Constitution Avenue, N.W., Washington, D.C. 20230.
Free. (N/M)

Slavic and East European Journal. Primarily analytical articles and
synthesizing studies on Slavic and East European languages, liter-
ature, and language pedagogy. Book reviews. Sample titles of re-
cent articles on literature: "The Magic Cards in The Queen of
Spades," "On the Poetics of Tolstoi's Confession," "Vololin's
Poems on the Evolution and Civil War." About 100 pages per issue.
Published quarterly by the American Association of Teachers of
Slavic and East European Languages (AATSEEL), Department of
Foreign Languages and Literatures, Northern Illinois University,
DeKalb, Illinois 00115. Obtainable from Joe Malik, Jr., Secretary-
Treasurer, Department of Russian and Slavic Studies, Modern Lan-
guages 340, University of Arizona, Tuscon, Arizona 85721. Free

to members of AATSEEL (membership dues, $15.00 per year; $7.50 for students for a maximum of three years); $4.50 per issue for nonmembers; $17.50 per year for libraries and institutions. (N/M) Since 1943.

Slavic Review. Primary emphasis on Russian, Soviet, and East European history, literature, and culture. Some articles on economics, politics, sociology, and related areas. Book reviews and book review articles take up about two-thirds of each issue. "Notes and Comments"; letters to the editor; "News of the Profession." Selected list of reference works on Slavic and East European topics. Sample titles of recent articles: "Peter I's Testament: 1965-73: A Reassessment," "Origins of the Russian Puppet Theater: An Alternative Hypothesis," "The Repluralization of Czechoslovak Politics in the 1960's." Averages about 225 pages per issue. Editorial office at 409 East Chalmers Street, Room 352, University of Illinois, Champaign, Illinois 61820. Published quarterly by, and obtainable from, the American Association for the Advancement of Slavic Studies (AAASS), 190 West 19th Avenue, Room 254, Ohio State University, Columbus, Ohio 43210. Free to AAASS members, who also receive the AAASS Newsletter (see separate entry for description) and the Directory of Members, published irregulary, once every two or three years. AAASS membership dues: $20.00 per year regular; $30.00 sustaining; $7.50 emeritus; $25.00 joint (two listings, one set of publications); $7.50 for students with U.S. mailing address; $10.00 for students with foreign mailing address; $6.50 for students at member institutions; $20.00 per year for nonmembers. (M; N/M) Since 1941.

Slavonic and East European Review. Articles on Slavic countries, focusing on history, literature, and linguistics. Book reviews. Sample titles of recent articles: "The Polish Minority in Lithuania, 1918-1926," "The Seagull's Second Symbolist Play-Within-the-Play," "Logaoedic Metres in the Lyric Poetry of Marina Isvestyeva." About 160 pages per issue. Published quarterly by Cambridge University Press, P.O. Box 92, London NW2 DB, England. Obtainable from Cambridge University Press, 32 East 57th Street, New York, N.Y. 10022. $32.50 per year for individuals; $47.50 for institutions. (N/M) Since 1922.

Smoloskyp Brochures and Booklets. Reports on Ukrainian individuals and groups of individuals allegedly arrested, tried, and imprisoned in the Soviet Union. Sample titles of recent brochures and booklets: "Svyatoslav Karavansky, Ukrainian Writer: More than 30 Years in Prison," "Imprisoned Scientists," "Women's Voices from Soviet Labor Camps." Varies in length, from 6 to 32 pages. Published irregularly by Smoloskyp, P.O. Box 6066, Patterson Station, Baltimore, Maryland 21231. Priced from 7 cents for a six-page brochure to $1.00 for a 32-page booklet. (N/M)

Social Sciences (formerly Social Sciences Today). Interdisciplinary periodical with articles and analyses in philosophy, history, economics, politics, sociology, law, philology, psychology, ethnography, and archeology. Most articles translated from Soviet periodicals; some original contributions. Reports on recent scientific conferences. Book reviews. Sample titles of recent articles: "Quantitative Methods in Historical Investigations," "Science, Technology, and Economic Growth in the 'Third World,'" "General Crisis of Capitalism: Its Present Manifestations." Averages about 275 pages per issue. Published quarterly by the USSR Academy of Sciences, 33/12 Arbat, Moscow 121002, USSR. Obtainable from Mezhdunarodnaya Kniga, Moscow G-200, USSR. $5.50 per year. (M) Since 1970.

Social Sciences and Eastern Europe (see Sociology and Eastern Europe).

Social Sciences Today (see Social Sciences).

Socialism: Theory and Practice. Translations, some in condensed form, from a wide variety of Soviet newspapers, magazines, and journals in the social sciences and the humanities. Declared purpose: to serve as "a digest of the political and theoretical press featuring the vital problems of Marxist-Leninist theory, the practice of socialist and communist construction, the peoples' struggle for peace, democracy and socialism, and world-wide ideological struggle." Sample titles of recent articles: "Soviet Foreign Policy: Basic Ideological Principles," "Socialism and Communism: Some Problems of Theory," "Soviet Economy: Facts and Fantasies." Book reviews. 160 pages per issue. Published monthly by the Novosti Press Agency Publishing House, Moscow, USSR. Editorial board at 2 Pushkin Square, Moscow, USSR. Obtainable from Mezhdunarodnaya Kniga, Moscow G-200, USSR. $5.00 per year. (M) Since 1961.

Socialist Thought and Practice. Articles on Marxist theory and ideology and on political, economic, and social events, conditions, developments, and problems in Yugoslavia and, secondarily, in other parts of the world. Both original contributions and materials translated from other Yugoslav publications. Book reviews. Sample titles of recent articles: "Marxism, Esthetics, Criticism," "The Vitality of Self-management [in Yugoslavia]," "Europe and the De-

veloping Countries." About 100 pages per issue. Published monthly at Trg Marksa i Engelsa 11, P.O. Box 576, 11000 Belgrade,
Yugoslavia. Also obtainable from Jugoslovenska Knijga, Trg Republike 5, 11000 Belgrade, Yugoslavia. $10.00 per year. (M)
Since 1961.

Sociology and Eastern Europe. Focus on East Europe. Announcements of relevant conferences, seminars, dissertations completed,
fellowships available, and other issues of interest to social scientists, and especially to sociologists, specializing in East Europe.
Declared purpose: to serve "members of the American Sociological
Association and other social scientists interested in East Central
and Southeastern Europe . . . providing current, topical and useful information on a range of subjects that will serve the interest
of the professional sociologist, in addition to creating information
channels for interested scholars and teachers." About eight pages
per issue. Published quarterly at the Department of Sociology,
Connecticut College, Box 1437, New London, Connecticut 06320.
Free. (N/M) (As this index goes to press, the publishers of Sociology and Eastern Europe are planning (1) to put the periodical on
a subscription basis, with exact charges yet to be determined; (2)
to expand coverage to include the Soviet Union; and (3) perhaps to
change the title to Social Sciences and Eastern Europe.)

Sofia News. Illustrated, general-interest type newspaper. Some emphasis on politics, culture, and tourism. Announcements of opera
performances, concerts, exhibitions, and so on. Sample titles of
recent articles: "Our Musicians and Singers Abroad," "Sofia Gets
New Look," "Miner Rises to Mine Director." Eight pages per issue. Published weekly by the Sofia Press Agency, 44 Patriarch
Evtimi Boulevard, Sofia, Bulgaria. $5.00 per year. (M)

Southeastern Europe. Interdisciplinary journal concerned with history
and social science topics specifically relating to one or more of
the following countries: Albania, Bulgaria, Greece, Romania, and
Yugoslavia. Occasional notes, translations, documents. Book reviews; professional news. Sample titles of recent articles: "Notes
on the Beginnings of Modern Serbian Literature: The Kurzbeck
Press in Vienna and Its Successors, 1770-1800," "Recent Studies
in Balkan History," "Small States and the Policy of Nonalignment:
The Yugoslav Position." About 100 to 125 pages per issue. Published twice a year (quarterly publication planned for the future)
by the University Center for International Studies (UCIS), University of Pittsburgh, 218 Oakland Avenue, Pittsburgh, Pennsylvania
15260. Obtainable from UCIS Publications Section, University

Center for International Studies, C-6 Mervis Hall, University of Pittsburgh, Pittsburgh, Pennsylvania 15260. $15.00 per year for institutions; $12.50 for faculty; $8.00 for full-time students. Lower prices to subscribers taking more than one UCIS journal. For more specific information on discounts, see UCIS Journals. (N/M) Since 1974.

Soviet Analyst. Newsletter reporting critically on political and economic events and conditions in the USSR and on Soviet foreign policy. Declares that it aims at forming "a bridge between academic studies and journalism." Sample titles of recent articles: "Soviet Academic Upheavals," "Soviet-Norwegian Friction in the Arctic," "Is Life More Joyful Comrades?" Eight pages per issue. Published every two weeks by Research Publications Services Ltd., Victoria Hall, Fingal Street, East Greenwich, London SE10 ORF, England. $70.00 per year. (N/M) Since 1972.

Soviet and East European Abstracts Series (see ABSEES).

Soviet and Eastern European Foreign Trade. Primarily unabridged translations from Soviet and East European scholarly journals and from collections of articles published in book form. Occasional relevant articles contributed by Western scholars or translated from Western journals (for example, from Osteuropa). Sample titles of recent articles: "New Forms of Joint Planning by COMECON Countries," "The USA in Economic Relations between East and West," "The Foreign Trade of the People's Republic of China with the Eastern European Countries, 1950-1969." Averages about 100 pages per issue. Published quarterly by the International Arts and Sciences Press, 901 North Broadway, White Plains, New York 10603. $70.00 per year for institutions; $20.00 for individuals associated with subscribing institutions. (M) Since 1965.

Soviet Booklets. Booklets on a wide variety of subjects, including Marxist-Leninist ideology, all aspects of life in the USSR, documents, and critical examinations of nonsocialist countries and of the policies of the People's Republic of China. Sample titles of recently published booklets: What Is Communism? Questions and Answers; Social Effects of the Scientific and Technological Revolution under Capitalism; Women in the Soviet Union. Published irregularly, about 30 to 50 booklets per year, by the Novosti Press Agency Publishing House, Moscow, USSR. Obtainable from Soviet Booklets, 3 Rosary Gardens, London, SW7, England (the Soviet Embassy in England). $7.00 per year. (The Soviet embassies in the United States [1706 18th Street, N.W., Washington, D.C. 20009] and Canada [400 Stewart Street, Ottawa, Ontario KIN6L2] mail out

Soviet booklets free, on request. However, their mailings seem
to be less comprehensive and much less regular than those of the
Soviet Embassy in London). (M)

Soviet Business and Economic Report (see Soviet Business & Trade).

Soviet Business & Trade (formerly Soviet Business and Economic Report). Concise information of special interest to Western business-
    men and women intent on doing business with the USSR. Records
    of transactions; news of upcoming contract talks, trade exhibitions,
    sales seminars, and technology agreements; systematic studies of
    Soviet industry and agriculture; late-breaking developments on Ca-
    pitol Hill, in the White House, and in the Soviet Union. Material
    is received from a variety of sources, including the Soviet news
    agency, Tass. Sample titles of recent articles: "Soviet-American
    Jet," "Worthington Agreement," "Assembly Lines to U.S.S.R."
    Eight pages per issue. Published every two weeks by Welt/Porter
    Publishing Company, 1511 K Street, N.W., Suite 316, Washington,
    D.C. 20005. $195.00 per year; $350.00 for two years; $495.00
    for three years. (M; N/M)

Soviet Education. Translations from Soviet journals, and occasionally
    from books, in the field of education. Entire issues devoted to a
    single topic, such as Rural Schooling, Medical School in the USSR,
    or The Teaching of Physics in Soviet Secondary Schools. Averages
    somewhat over 100 pages per issue. Published monthly by the In-
    ternational Arts and Sciences Press, 901 North Broadway, White
    Plains, New York 10603. $110.00 per year for institutions; $30.00
    for individuals associated with subscribing institutions. (M) Since
    1958.

Soviet Export. Illustrated periodical of Soviet foreign trade organiza-
    tions. Published every two months at Korp. 2,13 Ul. Kahovka,
    Moscow 113461, USSR. Free. (M) (No further information pro-
    cured.)

Soviet Film. Pictorial magazine. Articles on Soviet and non-Soviet
    films, actors and actresses, producers, and related topics. Re-
    views of all new feature films produced in the USSR (about 125 per
    year). Reports on international film festivals held in the USSR.
    Annual calendar of important dates in the history of Soviet cinema
    art. Sample titles of recent articles: "Lydia Smirnova: An Actress
    Dedicated to Searching," "A Directoral Debut by Natalia Bondar-
    chuk, Nikolay Burliaev, and Igor Khutsiev," "Some Thoughts on
    Problems of Children's Films: Both Entertaining and Serious."
    44 pages per issue. Published monthly in Moscow. Obtainable

from Mezhdunarodnaya Kniga, Moscow G-200, USSR. $5.50 per
year. (M) Since 1957.

Soviet Geography: Review and Translation. Translations of current
Soviet research articles on geography from the major Soviet scientific journals in the field. Extensive section entitled "New Notes"
on Soviet political and economic developments of interest to geo-
graphers. Some original essays and some discussion articles on
Soviet research contributed by Western scholars. These Western
contributions were expanded as of 1976 "in a further effort to stim-
ulate a dialogue between Soviet and English-speaking geogra-
phers." Book reviews; survey of Soviet geographic literature.
Sample titles of recent articles: "Toward a Unification of Concepts
and Terms Used in Integral Landscape Investigations," "Interre-
gional Migration Analysis," "The Population Dynamics of East
Siberia and Problems of Prediction." About 72 pages per issue.
Published ten times per year by Scripta Publishing Company in
cooperation with the American Geographical Society at 1511 K
Street, N.W., Washington, D.C. 20005. Editorial inquiries to
Dr. Theodore Shabad, Editor, Soviet Geography, 145 East 84th
Street, New York, N.Y. 10018. $75.00 per year. (M; N/M) Since
1960.

Soviet Jewish Affairs (replaces Bulletin of Soviet Jewish Affairs).
Articles on Jewish life and Jewish problems in the USSR and East
Europe; analyses of Soviet and East European developments as
they affect Jewish affairs. Book reviews; some pictures; letters
to the editor; documents; a six-month chronicle of events relating
to Jewish interests in that region. Sample titles of recent articles:
"Soviet Anti-Zionist Cartoons," "U.S. Trade and Russian Jewry,"
"Freedom of Emigration and Soviet Jewry." Averages 144 pages
per issue. Published twice a year by the Institute of Jewish Affairs,
13-16 Jacob's Well Mews, George Street, London, WIH SPD, England. $7.50 per year; $12.50 by airmail. (N/M) Since 1971.

Soviet Jewry Action Newsletter. Emphasis on alleged arrests, im-
prisonment, and oppression of Jews in the Soviet Union and pro-
posals for action (for instance, the mailing of thousands of post-
cards to Brezhnev). Two pages per issue. Published every three
weeks by Student Struggle for Soviet Jewry, 200 West 72nd Street,
Suites 30-31, New York, N.Y. 10023. $10.00 per year. (N/M)
Since 1969.

Soviet Land. Published twice a month by the Information Departments
of the USSR Embassy in India, 25 Barakhambra Road, New Delhi
1, India. Seven rupees per year. (M) (No other information procured.)

Soviet Law and Government. Unabridged translations of Soviet articles in the general area of law and government in the USSR. Sample titles of recent articles: "Party Organizations and Production
Associations," "The Economy and Economic Law," "The Present
Status of Soviet Copyright Law." About 150 pages per issue. Published quarterly by the International Arts and Sciences Press, 901
North Broadway, White Plains, New York 10603. $70.00 per year
for institutions; $20.00 for individuals associated with subscribing
institutions. (M) Since 1962.

Soviet Life (formerly USSR). Pictorial magazine. Covers all aspects
of life in the USSR, including ideology, history, economics, education, science, art, literature, and sports. Occasional articles on
other countries; section on queries from readers; children's corner; cartoons. Declared purpose: to provide "firsthand information
on the hopes, problems, aspirations, plans of the Soviet people."
Circulated in the United States by a reciprocal agreement between
the U.S. and Soviet governments under which this magazine is distributed in the United States by the Soviet Embassy in Washington,
D.C., and a magazine entitled Amerika is distributed in the Soviet
Union by the U.S. Embassy in Moscow. Sample titles of recent
articles: "The Mobility of Soviet Society," "Hockey, Russian Style,"
"Sergei Yesenin: Poetic Heart of Russia." About 64 pages per
issue. Published monthly by the Embassy of the Union of Soviet
Socialist Republics, 1706 Eighteenth Street, N.W., Washington,
D.C. 20009. $6.00 per year; $9.50 for two years; $14.50 for
three years. (M) Since 1956.

Soviet Literature. Selected pieces from Soviet literature, including
fiction, nonfiction, and poetry. Also literary news, comments,
analyses, and criticism; reports on the progress of the arts, art
reproductions. Letters to and from the editors. Sample titles of
recent articles: "The Islander" (a 90-page short story by Zoya
Zhuravloyova), "Leafing through Music Scores," "Young Faces
in Literature." 192 pages per issue. Published monthly by the
Writers Union of the USSR, 1/7 Kutuzovsky Prospect, Moscow
121248, USSR. $5.00 per year. (M) Since 1946.

Soviet Military Review. Illustrated military-political review. Focus
on theoretical and practical problems of the art of warfare, experience in the development of the Soviet armed forces, and questions of military pedagogics and psychology. Also articles on military history, especially the history of World War II and the Soviet
army's major operations, including reminiscences by prominent
Soviet military commanders. Some political articles; some fiction with military themes. Reviews of military literature published

in the USSR and abroad. Sample titles of recent articles: "Combined Army and Navy Operations," "A Battalion in a Seaborn Landing," "USA: Promises and Reality." 64 pages per issue. Published monthly by Krasnaya Zvezda Publishing House, Moscow, USSR. Obtainable from Mezhdunarodnaya Kniga, Moscow, G-200, USSR. $8.00 per year. (M)

Soviet News. News items and articles, usually translated or summarized from the Soviet press and Soviet news services. Sample titles of recent articles: "Nikolai Podgorny's Message to World Conference of Women," "Cosmonauts Continue Their Experiments on Salyut 4," "Rapid Rise in National Incomes and Output of COMECON Countries." Usually eight pages per issue. Published weekly by the Press Department of the Soviet Embassy, 3 Rosary Gardens, London SW7, England. Free. (M) Since 1941.

Soviet Panorama (formerly Soviet Union Today). Pictorial magazine. Focus on aspects of life in the USSR. Occasional articles on ideology and on other countries. Letters to the editor; cartoons; children's humor and children's stories. Sample titles of recent articles: "Industrial Output in Socialist and Capitalist Countries," "Bolshoi: For Two Centuries Its Magic Art Has Astounded the Admirers of Ballet and Opera," "International Tourism and the Freedom of the Individual." About 44 pages per issue. Published monthly by the Soviet Embassy in Canada, 400 Stewart Street, Ottawa, Ontario K1N 6L2, Canada. $3.00 per year requested but not required. (M) Since 1970.

Soviet Review (New Delhi). Published twice a week by the Information Department of the Soviet Embassy in India, 25 Barakhambra Road, New Delhi 1, India. Eight rupees per year. (M) (No other information procured.)

Soviet Review (United States). Reprints of selected articles previously published in the other 13 IASP journals that translate from Soviet sources. (For a list of those included in this index, see IASP Journals of Translations.) Declared purpose: "to provide a unique survey of recent work in the Soviet Union on economics, education, government, the humanities, psychology and psychiatry, and sociology. Drawing on all the disciplines and from an extraordinarily broad range of Soviet publications, this journal helps the reader assess the quality and variety of work being done by scholars in all centers of learning throughout the USSR." Sample titles of recent articles: "Public Education, Science, and Culture in the USSR," "Manpower and Labor Productivity," "Basic Principles in the Rehabilitation of Psychiatric Patients." About 100 pages per issue.

Published quarterly by the International Arts and Sciences Press, 901 North Broadway, White Plains, New York 10603. $12.00 per year. (M) Since 1970.

Soviet Sociology. Unabridged translations of Soviet articles on sociology taken from a wide variety of Soviet journals and books. Sample titles of recent articles: "Mixed Marriages in the Central Asian Republics and Kazakhstan in the 1930's," "Population Movement and Labor Supply in Siberia," "Women in the USSR: Statistical Data." Somewhat over 100 pages per issue. Published quarterly by the International Arts and Sciences Press, 901 North Broadway, White Plains, New York 10603. $70.00 per year for institutions; $20.00 for individuals associated with subscribing institutions. (M) Since 1962.

Soviet Statutes and Decisions. Unabridged translations of Soviet legal statutes and decisions. Each volume, consisting of four quarterly issues, concentrates on one aspect of Soviet law. Sample titles of recent volumes: Soviet Conservation Law, Soviet Administration of Legality, Soviet Maritime Law. Published quarterly by the International Arts and Sciences Press, 901 North Broadway, White Plains, N.Y. 10603. $70.00 per year for institutions; $20.00 for individuals associated with subscribing institutions. (M) Since 1964.

Soviet Studies. Analyses of social, political, economic, and cultural institutions, developments, and policies in the USSR. Some articles on socialist countries in East Europe. Book reviews. Sample titles of recent articles: "Functions of the Supreme Soviet Presidia and Standing Committees," "The End of the Russian Peasantry," "Polish Postwar Economic Growth." About 165 pages per issue. Published quarterly at the Institute of Soviet and East European studies of the University of Glasgow, Glasgow G12 8QG, Scotland. $23.50 per year. Joint annual subscription to SOVIET STUDIES and ABSEES (see above) at concessional joint rate (was $45.00 per year in 1976). Special joint rate for NASEES (National Association for Soviet and East European Studies) members and bona fide students (was $21.00 per year in 1976). (N/M) Since 1949.

Soviet Studies in History. Translations from Soviet journals on history, primarily but not exclusively from Voprosy historii and Istoria SSSR. Described by the publisher as consisting of "major studies by [Soviet] historians and historiographers, chosen to reflect the broad range of Soviet interests." Sample titles of recent articles: "On the Subject of Historiographic Research," "The American and the French Revolutions of the Eighteenth Century (An

Attempt at a Comparative Characterization)," "The Teaching of Contemporary History in the Universities." Averages slightly under 100 pages per issue. Published quarterly by the International Arts and Sciences Press, 901 North Broadway, White Plains, New York 10603. $70.00 per year for institutions; $20.00 for individuals associated with subscribing institutions. (M) Since 1962.

Soviet Studies in Literature. Translations from Soviet literary journals of articles on literary history, theory, criticism, and controversy covering prerevolutionary and Soviet works. Sample titles of recent articles: "Unknown Articles by Vladimir Mayakovsky on the Film," "The Solzhenitsyn Controversy," "Pushkin." Published quarterly by the International Arts and Sciences Press, 901 North Broadway, White Plains, New York 10603. Averages about 100 pages per issue. $70.00 per year for institutions; $20.00 for individuals associated with subscribing institutions. (M) Since 1964-65.

Soviet Studies in Philosophy. Unabridged translations from Soviet philosophical journals, primarily from Voprosy filosofii. An entire issue is often devoted to a single topic, such as "The Forming of the New Person: Philosophical Problems of Education and Socialization," "Philosophers of the German Democratic Republic," and "Philosophical Problems of Ecology." Averages somewhat over 100 pages per issue. Published quarterly by the International Arts and Sciences Press, 901 North Broadway, White Plains, New York 10603. $70.00 per year for institutions; $20.00 for individuals associated with subscribing institutions. (M) Since 1962.

Soviet Union (Moscow). Illustrated magazine. Deals with all aspects of Soviet life. Declared purpose: "to familiarize the foreign reader with the life and work of Soviet people, with the USSR's policies, its economy, science, technology, art and sports." Short stories; excerpts from works of fiction; reproductions of paintings by Soviet artists; interviews; questionnaires; letters to the editor; material prepared at the request of readers. Sample titles of recent articles: "Soyuz-Apollo: Before and After," "The Socialist Way of Life and National Consciousness," "Rembrandt in the Museums of the Soviet Union." About 57 pages per issue. Published monthly at 8 Ulitsa Moskvina, Moscow K-31, USSR. Obtainable from Mezhdunarodnaya Kniga, Moscow G-200, USSR. $5.00 per year. (M) Since 1950.

Soviet Union (University of Pittsburgh). Interdisciplinary journal concerned with current history and with social science topics, including

material about nationality and minority groups, relevant to the
USSR. Occasional notes, translations, documents. Book reviews;
professional news. Sample titles of recent articles: "Pravda and
Trud: Divergent Soviet Attitudes towards the Middle East," "Khru-
shchev and the Yemeni Revolution (1962-1964): An Analysis of So-
viet Policy and Attitudes," "Divorce in the USSR: Spatial and Legal
Changes, 1940-60." About 100 to 125 pages per issue. Published
twice a year (quarterly publication planned for the future) by the
University Center for International Studies (UCIS), University of
Pittsburgh, 218 Oakland Avenue, Pittsburgh, Pennsylvania 15260.
Obtainable from UCIS Publications Section, University Center for
International Studies, C-6 Mervis Hall, University of Pittsburgh,
Pittsburgh, Pennsylvania 15260. $15.00 per year for institutions;
$12.50 for faculty; $8.00 for full-time students; lower prices to
subscribers taking more than one UCIS journal. For more specific
information on discounts, see UCIS Journals. (N/M) Since 1974.

Soviet Union Today (see Soviet Panorama).

Soviet Weekly. Illustrated newspaper. Features news items and articles on economic, political, and social life and on sports and culture in the Soviet Union. Sections on "People in the News" and
"World Affairs." Book reviews. Chess problems, stamp column.
Sample titles of recent articles: "Academy of Sciences Celebrates
250 Years," "Gromyko at UN: Peaceful Co-existence the Way Forward," "British-Soviet Health Pact Goes Ahead." 16 pages per
issue. Published weekly by Soviet Weekly, 3 Rosary Gardens,
London SW7 4NW, England (the Soviet Embassy in England). $10.00
per year. (M) Since 1942.

Soviet World Outlook. Emphasis on presentation and analysis of Moscow's views on international issues as revealed in authoritative
Soviet sources. Declared purpose: "to report monthly on Kremlin
views critically affecting U.S. interests: examine Soviet statements
as key to understanding Soviet actions; seek to inject Kremlin's
views into U.S. debate on Relations with the USSR." Sample titles
of recent articles: "Soviets Push Struggle for Economic Supremacy,"
"Moscow Eyes Revolutionary Prospects in West and Searches for
More Effective Strategy and Tactics," "Moscow Deplores U.S.
Failure to Understand and Give Due Weight to Soviet Views on Re-
laxation in U.S.-Soviet Relations." Eight to ten pages per issue.
Published monthly by the Current Affairs Press for the Center for
Advanced International Studies, University of Miami, 1730 Rhode
Island Avenue, N.W., Washington, D.C. 20036. $48.00 per year
for institutions; $18.00 (prepaid) for individuals at home addresses.
(N/M) Since 1976.

Soviet Woman. Pictorial magazine. Primary focus on the Soviet woman—her status, her economic and public activities, her growing importance in all spheres of Soviet life. Also articles on the position of women in capitalist, developing, and in other socialist countries. Some articles on family life, child rearing, and the arts and literature. A children's story in each issue. Sample titles of recent articles: "Education: That Is How Equality Is Attained," "Fifteen Years on the Court," "Women Demand Peace and Disarmament." About 40 pages per issue. Published monthly by the Soviet Women's Committee and the Central Council of Trade Unions of the USSR, Kuznetsky Most 22, Moscow, USSR. Obtainable from Mezhdunarodnaya Kniga, Moscow G-200, USSR. $5.00 per year. (M) Since 1945.

Sport. Illustrated magazine. Focus on student sports news with special emphasis on international events. In some issues, multipage spread of sports and camping activities of the International Union of Students. Text in English, French, and Spanish. Sample titles of recent articles: "1st European Student Cycling Championship," "World Student Judo Championship," "1st International Student Sports Camp in Czechoslovakia." About 30 to 40 pages per issue. Published every two months by the Physical Education and Sports Department of the International Union of Students, 17th November Street, P.O. Box 58, 110 01 Prague 01, Czechoslovakia. Free. (M)

Sport in the USSR. Illustrated magazine. Articles on all aspects of sports life in the USSR and on competitive sports events. Frequent stories about outstanding Soviet sportsmen and women. Sample titles of recent articles: "Science and Sport" (a report on the World Scientific Congress on "Sport in Modern Society" held in Moscow), "From PWD [Prepared for Work and Defense] Badge to Olympic Medal," "South-African Racists Must be Banned from World Sport." About 32 pages per issue. Published monthly by Soviet Union magazine, 8 Ulitsa Moscvina, Moscow 103772. Obtainable from Mezhdunarodnaya Kniga, Moscow G-200, USSR. $3.50 per year. (M) Since 1966.

Sports in Romania. Illustrated magazine. Focus on Romanian participation in world sports events and especially in the Olympics. Sample titles of recent articles: "Romanian Sportsmen and Sportswomen in the 1975 World Championships," "Romania in the Winter Olympic Games," "The Romanian Ice Hockey Team in Full Rejuvenation Process." 32 pages per issue. Published quarterly by the Romanian Olympic Committee, Vasile Conta St., Bucharest, Romania. $8.00 per year. (M) Since 1958.

Sputnik. Selected articles translated from newspapers and magazines
    throughout the USSR. Some pieces reproduced in full, but most in
    condensed form. Covers all areas of life in the USSR, from ideol-
    ogy, economics, politics, and international relations to sports,
    fashions, and memoirs. Also articles on other countries. Pictures
    and art reproductions; recipes; humor. Letters to the editor; edi-
    tors' replies to questions. Declared purpose: "to provide the reader
    with information about what is going on in our country [the USSR],
    drawing on the whole diversity of the Soviet press for this purpose."
    Sample titles of recent articles: "A New Star in Mathematics,"
    "Introducing the Moscow Zoo," "Liberation of Romania." 176
    pages per issue. Published monthly by the Soviet Press Agency
    APN, 2 Pushkin Square, Moscow, USSR. $5.50 per year. (M)
    Since 1967.

Sputnik Junior. Published monthly by the Information Department of
    the Embassy of the USSR, Soviet Land Office, 25 Barakhamba
    Road, New Delhi 1, India. Five rupees per year. (M) (No further
    information procured.)

Statistical Yearbook (UNESCO). Detailed statistical information on
    all aspects of education, science and technology, and culture and
    communication. Covers more than 200 countries, including all the
    socialist countries. Text in English and French. Published yearly
    by the UNESCO Press, 7 Place de Fontenoy, 75700 Paris, France.
    Distributed in the United States by UNIPUB, Box 433, Murray Hill
    Station, New York, N.Y. 10016. Price varies; the 1974 edition
    for instance, published in December 1975, was $60 per issue.
    (M; N/M)

Statistical Yearbook (United Nations). Detailed and extensive infor-
    mation on production, consumption, transportation, finance, na-
    tional accounts, health, housing, education, and so on. Covers
    some 200 countries, including the socialist countries. However,
    statistical information on some, such as mainland China, Mongolia,
    and North Korea, is at times unavailable, so that even world totals
    sometimes specifically exclude these countries. Published annually.
    Obtainable from United Nations Publications, LX 2300, New York,
    N.Y. 10017. Price varies; the 1974 issue was $30.00 in paper-
    back and $38.00 clothbound. (M; N/M)

Statistical Yearbook for Asia and the Pacific. Statistical information
    on a wide variety of subjects, including population, manpower, na-
    tional accounts, agriculture, forestry and fishing, industry, energy
    supplies, consumption, transportation and communication, inter-
    nal trade, external trade, wages, prices and household expenditures,

and financial and social statistics. Covers most of the countries
of Asia, including the socialist countries of China, Laos, Mongolia, North Korea, and Vietnam. Over 450 pages per issue. Published annually by the U.N. Economic and Social Commission for
Asia and the Pacific, Bangkok, Thailand. Obtainable from United
Nations Publications, LX2300, New York, N.Y. 10017. Price
varies; the 1974 issue was $20.00. (N/M)

Statni Banka Ceskoslovenska: Bulletin. Detailed reports on economic
conditions and developments in Czechoslovakia; special emphasis
on monetary, financial, and credit matters. Verbal descriptions
supplemented by extensive statistical information presented in the
form of tables and graphs. Primary emphasis on the preceding
year; some tables and graphs cover the past four or five years, a
few the past 15 years. About 38 pages per issue. Published annually by Statni Banka Ceskoslovenska (State Bank of Czechoslovakia),
Prague, Czechoslovakia. Free. (M)

Studies (see Studies and Documents).

Studies and Documents. Booklets on various aspects of Yugoslav politics, economics, and current events. Each booklet devoted to
one topic; some are in the Documents and some in the Studies
series. Sample titles of recent Documents booklets: Five Years
of the Social and Economic Reform in Yugoslavia, Yugoslav Atti-
tude to the Policy of Active Peaceful Coexistence. Sample titles
of recent Studies booklets: The Socio-Political System of Yugoslavia, Economic Development of Yugoslavia. Averages around 50
pages per booklet. Both series are published irregularly, Studies
by the Federal Committee for Information, Mose Pijade 8 Belgrade, Yugoslavia, and Documents by Medunarodna Kniga, Nemanjina 34, P.O. Box 413, Belgrade, Yugoslavia. Obtainable from
Medunarodna Politika, 34 Nemanjina, P.O. Box 413, Belgrade,
Yugoslavia. $3.00 per year for both series together. (M)

Studies in Comparative Communism. Interdisciplinary journal. Primary emphasis on comparative studies of Communist parties, systems, policies, and related topics. Documents; book review articles. Sample titles of recent articles: "A Comparison of the Current Chinese and Soviet Central Committees," "Communist Systems and Modernization: Sources of Political Crises," "The New
Togetherness: American and Soviet Reactions." About 100 pages
per issue. Published quarterly by the Von KleinSmid Institute for
International Affairs, School of International Relations, University
of Southern California, University Park, Los Angeles, California

90007. $10.00 per year for individuals; $16.00 for institutions.
(N/M) Since 1968.

Studies in Soviet Thought. Journal devoted primarily to the publication of articles and research papers on Marxist-Leninist philosophy,
with special emphasis on contemporary Soviet thought. Book reviews. Sample titles of recent articles: "The Soviet Onslaught on
Mao Tsetung Thought: The Rumjancev School," "Some Observations
on the Alleged Classicism of Socialist Realism," "The Soviet Union
Then and Now: Some Recent Publications on the Soviet Union."
Averages about 90 pages per issue. Published quarterly by the In-
stitute of East-European Studies at the University of Fribourg
(Switzerland), the Center for East Europe, Russia and Asia at
Boston College, and the Seminar for Political Theory and Philoso-
phy at the University of Munich. Editorial office for the United
States at the Department of Philosophy, Boston College, Chestnut
Hill, Massachusetts 02167. Obtainable from D. Reidel Publishing
Company, P.O. Box 17, Dordrecht, Holland. 90 Dutch florins per
year plus 15 florins per year for postage and handling. (N/M)

Studies on the Developing Countries. Focus on topics related to the
political, economic, and social conditions, problems, and development of less developed countries. Book reviews. Sample titles of
recent articles: "Economic Growth and Social Progress (Facts
about and Prospects for Developing Countries)," "Economic Integration in Latin America," "Socialist Industrialization and Under-
development: Polish Experience and Its Strategic Implications for
Developing Countries." About 165 pages per issue. Published
twice a year by the Polish Institute for International Affairs, la
Warecka Street, P.O. Box 1000, 00-950 Warsaw, Poland. $5.00
per year. Also obtainable on an exchange basis for publications on
contemporary international subjects. (M) Since 1972.

Summary of World Broadcasts (SWB) (see B.B.C. Monitoring Service).

Survey. Emphasis on political, economic, and, to a somewhat lesser
extent, social and cultural conditions and developments in the Soviet Union and East Europe. Sample titles of recent articles: "Top
Incomes in the USSR: Towards a Definition of the Soviet Elite,"
"Rumania: Background to Autonomy," "The Theater of the Absurd
in Czechoslovakia." About 200 pages per issue. Usually published
quarterly (occasionally one issue for two quarters) under the auspices of the International Association for Cultural Freedom and
Stanford University by the Oxford University Press, Ilford House,
133 Oxford Street, London WIR ITD, England. Obtainable from
Subscription Department, Oxford University Press, Press Road,

Neasden NW10, England. $16.00 per year; $8.00 for students. (N/M) Since 1955.

Ta Kung Pao Weekly Supplement. Newspaper focusing on news items concerning China and conditions and developments in China. Occasional articles on other countries. Section entitled "In Brief" consisting of short news items from around the world. Sections entitled "Visiting the Country" and "Leaving for Abroad" cover visits of VIPs and delegations to and from China. "What the Press Says" gives translations of brief items from the press of other countries, such as Albania, Mexico, Ethiopia, and Thailand. Letters to the editor. Some pictures, with an occasional special multipage pictorial insert, recently, for instance, on Chou En-lai. Sample titles of recent articles: "Chairman Mao Meets Dr. Kissinger," "New Artificial Larynxes for Patients to Regain Vocalization," "Soviet Economy Heads for Total Militarization." 16 pages per issue. Published weekly at 342 Hennessy Road, 7th floor, Hong Kong. $10.00 per year; $19.00 by air freight, redirected by Ta Kung Pao's Vancouver agent; $55.00 by airmail directly to subscriber. (M)

TANJUG Features. Translations of feature articles published by TANJUG, the Yugoslav wire service. Covers all aspects of Yugoslav affairs and life in Yugoslavia, including economic, political, and social developments; foreign relations; tourism; sports; cultural events; ecology; and human interest stories. Each issue devoted to one topic. Sample titles of recent issues: New Railway Connects Belgrade with the Adriatic, Successful Conference of the Unaligned, A Successful Year in Yugoslav Athletics. Two to three pages per issue. Published continuously, several issues per month, by TANJUG, Obilicev venac 2, Belgrade, Yugoslavia 11000. Free. (M)

Théâtre en Pologne/Theatre in Poland. Illustrated magazine. Emphasis on news of the Polish theater. Book reviews; play reviews. Side-by-side French and English text. Sample titles of recent articles: "Boy-Zelenski's Role in 20th Century Polish Culture," "25 Years of the Jewish Theater in People's Poland," "Pen-Portrait of an Actor, Wojciech Pszoniak." 48 pages per issue. Published monthly by the Polish Center of the International Theatre Institute, Ul. Moliera 1, 00-072 Warsaw, Poland. $19.80 per year. (M) Since 1958.

Trade and Tours. Pictorial magazine. Focus on topics relevant to China's international economic relations and particularly to the exportation of Chinese products. Special emphasis on trade fairs and primarily on the Canton Trade Fair. Advertisements of products China offers for sale abroad. Some art reproductions. Half in English, half in Chinese. Sample titles of recent articles: "The Development of China's Shipbuilding Industry," "China's Latest Handicrafts," "China's Rare Animals." About 120 pages per issue. Published twice a year by Trade and Service Press, 15th floor, Kwok Wah Building, 342 Hennessy Road, Hong Kong. $1.25 per issue. (M)

Trade Unions of Romania. Illustrated magazine. Emphasis on youth, workers, working conditions, labor unions, and general political and economic developments in Romania. Section entitled "From the International Activity of Romanian Trade Unions." Some advertisements of products Romania offers for sale abroad. Sample titles of recent articles: "About Young People and Their Early Steps into Factories," "Trade Union Life: How a Tradition Begins," "Medical Assistance in Enterprises." About 36 pages per issue. Published quarterly by the Central Council of Trade Unions of the Socialist Republic of Romania, 14 Strade Stefan Gheorghiu, Sectorul 1, Bucharest, Romania. $8.00 per year. (M) Since 1961.

Translation Service. Translations from the Yugoslav press, with primary emphasis on politics and economics. Two- to three-page section listing headlines from Yugoslavia's two leading dailies, Borba and Politika. Sample titles of recent articles: "Report from [Yugoslav] Trade Unions," "Yugoslav-Italian Relations: An Example to the World," "Foreign Exchange Inflow from Tourism Over One Milliard [billion] Dollars." Averages about 20 pages per issue. Occasional supplements of varying length usually consisting of translations of new laws or other important documents, for example, "Draft Bases of Common Policy of Yugoslavia's Long-Term Development until 1985" (114 pages). Published daily except Sunday (combined issue for Sunday and Monday) by the British Embassy in Belgrade, Yugoslavia, under the auspices of a board drawn from members of embassies of all European Economic Community countries in Belgrade. Obtainable directly from editor, whose name appears on the front page of each issue (currently V. Jovanovic, 42 Generala Zdanova, 11000 Belgrade, Yugoslavia); or send inquiries to British Embassy, Belgrade, Yugoslavia. 525 dinars per month. Supplements sold separately; price dependent upon length (the one mentioned above, for instance, costs 300 dinars). (M)

Translations of People's Republic of China Press. Covers all aspects of Chinese affairs and life in China, including Chinese industry, agriculture, mining, sports, Communist party ideology, political

activity, foreign affairs, and views on international events. Includes three series:

1. Survey of Chinese newspapers; published weekly; approximately
   300 pages
2. Magazine selections from nontechnical Chinese publications; published monthly; approximately 300 pages
3. Background briefs compiled from varied Chinese sources

   All translations are prepared by the U.S. Consulate General in
   Hong Kong. Subscription includes a quarterly subject index. Ob-
   tainable from U.S. Department of Commerce, National Technical
   Information Service (NTIS), 5285 Port Royal Road, Springfield,
   Virginia 22151. $275.00 per year. (M)

Travel to the USSR. Pictorial magazine. Focus on issues of interest
   to tourists visiting the USSR, including occasional articles on Soviet history and ideology. Sections entitled "Travel to the USSR
   suggests: Where to Go and What to See" (brief, one-paragraph descriptions of cities, interesting places, and other tourist attractions); "Diary and Events" (reports on exhibitions, conferences,
   visiting tourist groups, openings of new airline services, and so
   on); "Our Guests Comment" (comments by tourists on their visits
   to the USSR). Announcements of plays, movies, and sports events.
   Sample titles of recent articles: "Moscow's Red Square," "Monuments to War Heroes," "International Women's Year in the Soviet
   Union." 48 pages per issue. Published every two months at 8
   Neglinnaya ulitsa, Moscow D-31, USSR. Obtainable from Mezhdunarodnaya Kniga, Moscow G-200, USSR. $2.00 per year. (M)
   Since 1966.

Trends in Communist Media. Analyzes Chinese, Soviet, and other
   Communist media discussions of key issues under a confidential
   classification limited to six months. Describes Communist media
   in the perspective of past content and behavior; identifies new ele-
   ments or departures from the standard line; assesses the impact
   of changes. Occasional supplementary articles on subjects deemed
   of continuing longer-range interest. Averages 20 to 30 pages per
   issue. The declassified Trends are made available weekly by
   Foreign Broadcast Information Service, P.O. Box 2604, Washington, D.C. 20013. Obtainable from U.S. Department of Commerce,
   National Technical Information Service (NTIS), 5285 Port Royal
   Road, Springfield, Virginia 22161. $60.00 per year. (N/M)

Trends in World Economy. Hungarian booklets on various economic
   topics. Samples of recent titles: The CMEA Countries on the Road

to Economic Integration, Economic Growth and the Development
Level, Recent Trends in the Industrialization of the Developing
Countries and the Global Strategy of the Leading Capitalist Countries. Some booklets in English, others in French, Russian, Spanish, German, and Hungarian. Published irregularly by the Hungarian Scientific Council for World Economy, Kallo Esperes u. 15,
P.O. Box 36, Budapest 126, Hungary. Price and frequency of publication not given. (M)

Tricontinental. Articles on political, social, and economic conditions
and developments in Africa, Asia and Latin America, analyzed
from a Marxist-Leninist point of view. Some illustrations; book
reviews. Sample titles of recent articles: "On the Reunification of
Korea," "South Africa: The Other Imperialism," "San Salvador:
Culture Behind Bars." Averages about 150 pages per issue. Published every two months by the Executive Secretariat of the Organization of Solidarity of the Peoples of Africa, Asia, and Latin America, P.O. Box 4224, Havana, Cuba. $3.60 per year. (M) Since
1967.

Twentieth Century and Peace. Illustrated magazine. Emphasis on
peaceful coexistence; disarmament; nuclear nonproliferation; responsibility of scientists to prevent use of scientific discoveries
for destructive purposes; economic, cultural, and scientific ties
among countries; and related topics. Reports on activities of both
local Soviet and international peace organizations. Occasional articles on "national liberation" struggles. Letters to the editor;
questions by readers and answers by the editors. Sample titles of
recent articles: "On Problems of Universal and Complete Disarmament," "Europe—A Continent of Peace," "Palestinians Fight for
Their Rights." About 30 to 50 pages per issue. Published monthly
by Moscow News, 16/2 Gorky Street, Moscow, USSR. Obtainable
from Mezhdunarodnaya Kniga, Moscow G-200, USSR. $1.50 per
year. (M) Since 1974.

UCIS Journals. The University Center for International Studies (UCIS)
at the University of Pittsburgh publishes six journals: Byzantine
Studies, Canadian-American Slavic Studies, East Central Europe,
Russian History, Southeastern Europe, and Soviet Union. Five of
these are described in this index under their respective titles;
Byzantine Studies does not properly belong in this index. (Another
UCIS periodical, Cuban Studies, published at the UCIS Center for
Latin American Studies, is described in this index but is not included here as being among those for which multiple-purchase dis-
counts are given.) UCIS offers the following prices and discounts
to subscribers:

Number of Journals Subscribed To	Faculty and In- dividuals	Students	Institutions*
One journal only	$ 12.50	$ 8.00	$ 15.00
Any two journals	20.00	13.00	24.00
Any three journals	32.50	21.00	39.00
Any four journals	38.00	24.00	48.00
Any five journals	47.50	30.00	63.00
All six journals	57.00	36.00	67.50

*Discounts are granted only to institutions not ordering through an agent; agents receive a 20 percent discount rate.

All journals are obtainable from UCIS Publications Section, University Center for International Studies, C-6 Mervis Hall, University of Pittsburgh, Pittsburgh, Pennsylvania 15260. (N/M)

Ukraine. Pictorial magazine. Articles on the development of the Ukrainian Republic's economy; Ukrainian achievements in the fields of science, technology, culture, art, and education; and the U- kraine's forests, steppes, rivers, fauna, and flora. Excerpts from new works of Ukrainian fiction; humorous stories; poems; art reproductions; cartoons. Occasional articles on other parts of the USSR and on international topics. 24 pages per issue. Pub- lished quarterly by Soviet Ukraine Publishers, 4 Petr Nesterov Street, 252047 Kiev, Ukraine, USSR. Obtainable from Mezhdunaro- dnaya Kniga, Moscow G-200, USSR. $1.20 per year. (M) Since 1974.

Ukrainian Quarterly. Articles dealing primarily with political, social, economic, and cultural problems of the Ukraine and secondarily with the rest of the USSR and East Europe. "Chronicle of Current Events" divided into "Ukrainian Life in the United States," "Ukrain- ians in the Diaspora," and "In Captive Ukraine." Pertinent docu- ments. Book reviews. Sample titles of recent articles: "The Ukrainian-Jewish Problem: A Historical Retrospect," "Problems of the Non-Russian Peoples as Exemplified by Recent Ukrainian Publications," "The Despairing West and the Confident East." About 110 to 120 pages per issue. Published quarterly at 302-304 West 13th Street, New York, N.Y. 10014. $9.00 per year. (N/M) Since 1944.

Ukrainian Review (London). Illustrated magazine of news, culture, and life in the Ukraine. Published quarterly by the Association of Ukrainians in Great Britain, Ltd., 49 Linden Gardens, London W2, England. $7.00 per year. (N/M) Since 1954.

Ukrainian Review (New York) (replaces monthly Anglo-Ukrainian News). Focus on the life and affairs of Ukrainians in the Ukrainian Republic, elsewhere in the USSR, and abroad. Main slant illustrated by the magazine's front-page request to "release from Soviet prisons and concentration camps all Ukrainians . . . and all those punished for demanding human rights and national independence." Sample titles of recent articles: "Appeal of the Fifth Congress of Ukrainian Nationalists to the Freedom-Loving Nations," "The Anniversary of Ukraine's Independence," "Ukrainian Poetry in Canada: A Historical Account." About 95 pages per issue. Published quarterly by the Association of Ukrainians in Great Britain, Ltd., 49 Linden Gardens, London W2 4HG. U.S. representative: Organization for Defense of Four Freedoms for Ukraine, P.O. Box 304, Cooper Station, New York, N.Y. 10003. $8.00 per year. (N/M) Since 1954.

UNESCO Statistical Yearbook (see Statistical Yearbook [UNESCO]).

Union of Yugoslav Youth. Newsletter (supersedes Youth Life). Illustrated magazine. Emphasis on topics of interest to Yugoslavia's youth. Book reviews; film reviews. Published monthly by the Union of Yugoslav Youth, Bulevar Lenijina 11070 Belgrade, Yugoslavia. Free. (M) Since 1971.

United Nations Statistical Yearbook (see Statistical Yearbook [United Nations]).

U.S. Bureau of East-West Trade Office of Export Administration, Export Administration Report (formerly U.S. Bureau of East-West Trade Office of Export Administration. Quarterly Report—Export Controls). Report on U.S. export controls to the president and Congress. Published twice a year by the U.S. Department of Commerce, Office of Export Administration, Washington, D.C. 20230. (N/M) Since 1947.

U.S. Bureau of East-West Trade Office of Export Administration. Quarterly Report—Export Controls (see U.S. Bureau of East-West Trade Office of Export Administration, Export Administration Report).

U.S. China Business Review. Illustrated magazine aimed at providing practical guidance, assistance, and information for companies developing trade with China. Emphasis on importing from, and exporting to, China and on sectors of the Chinese economy. Occasional statistical data. Sections entitled "Exporter's Notes," "Importer's Notes," "China Economic Notes," "China Trade Events," "International China Notes." Book reviews. Sample titles of recent articles: "How Chinese Goods Are Marketed in Great Britain,"

"China's Mini-Fairs 1976—Demand Meets Supply," "China's Merchant Marine." About 60 pages per issue. Published every two months by the National Council for United States-China Trade, 1050 Seventeenth Street, N.W., Washington, D.C. 20036. $60.00 per year; $50.00 for libraries. (N/M) Since 1974.

U.S.-China Peoples Friendship Association Pamphlet Series. Pamphlets, each devoted to one specific topic relevant to understanding and friendship between the United States and China. Sample titles of recent issues: Opium and China, The Taiwan Question: Roadblock to Friendship? 15 to 20 pages per pamphlet. Published irregularly, two to three pamphlets per year, by the U.S.-China Peoples Friendship Association, National Office, 2700 West Third Street, Room 102, Los Angeles, California 90057. 25 cents per pamphlet. (N/M)

U.S. Trade Status with Socialist Countries. Primarily statistical tables showing U.S. trade with the USSR, China, the People's Republic of Mongolia, and each of the socialist countries of East Europe, except Yugoslaiva, which the U.S. Department of Commerce treats as a "Western" country. Separate tables show exports to, and imports from, each of the countries covered, broken down into ten commodity categories, for the past two or three years. About 14 pages per issue. Published monthly by the Trade Analysis Division, Bureau of East-West Trade, U.S. Department of Commerce, Washington, D.C. 20230. Free. (N/M)

USSR (see Soviet Life.)

USSR and the Third World. Survey of Soviet and Chinese relations with Africa, Asia, and Latin America. All short items, usually one, at most three, paragraphs in length. Each issue divided into "Military," "Political, Diplomatic and Cultural," and "Economic and Scientific." Each of these sections subdivided geographically into Asia, Middle East, Africa, and Latin America. Each of the geographic regions further subdivided into countries, and each country has a section on relations with and reports from the USSR, and another on relations with and reports from China. Averages about 50 pages per issue. Published eight times per year by the Central Asian Research Center, 1B Parkfield Street, London, N1 OPR, England. $50.00 per year; airmail charges extra. (M; N/M)

Vietnam. Pictorial magazine. Focus on all aspects of life in Vietnam, recently with some emphasis on the war in Vietnam and on the victory. Occasional "Children's Corner" and letters to the editor. Sample titles of recent articles: "Splendid Victory—Radiant Future," "Learning within Reach of All," "The Ethnic Minorities in Vietnam."

About 28 pages per issue. Published monthly at 79 Ly Thuong Kiet, Hanoi, Socialist Republic of Vietnam. Obtainable from Xunhasaba, 32 Hai Ba Trung Street, Hanoi, Socialist Republic of Vietnam. $7.20 per year. (M) Since 1966.

Vietnam Courier. Focus on life in Vietnam, both North and South, recently with emphasis on the war in Vietnam, the victory, and the unification of Vietnam. Occasional articles and reports related to the progress of communism elsewhere. Includes two-page day-by-day chronology of news events. Sample titles of recent articles: "Talking with Former Puppet Officers," "Women's Rights in the Democratic Republic of Vietnam," "The U.S. War of Aggression in Cambodia: Chronology (March 1970-April 1975)." Published monthly by Vietnam Courier, Hanoi, Socialist Republic of Vietnam. Obtainable from Peace Book Company, 9-10 Queen Victoria Street, Hong Kong. $6.00 per year. (M)

Vietnam Youth. Illustrated magazine. Primary emphasis on problems and achievements of Vietnamese youth. Published quarterly by the Vietnam Youth Federation, 64 Ba Trieu Street, Hanoi, Socialist Republic of Vietnam. Free. (M) Since 1968.

Vietnamese Trade Unions Review. Reports of trade union activities in Vietnam and of events of special interest to members of Vietnamese trade unions. Sample titles of recent articles: "The Viet Nam National Union of Engineering and Metallurgical Workers," "Our Revolution's New Stage and the Trade Union Movement," "North Vietnam Reconstructs." 30 to 35 pages per issue. Published every two months by the Vietnam Federation of Trade Unions (TCD), 82 Tran Hung Dao Avenue, Hanoi, Socialist Republic of Vietnam. Price not given. (M)

Weekly Bulletin. News bulletin with emphasis on economic, political, and cultural developments in Hungary. "News in Brief" and "Last Week's Events" consist of two pages of one-paragraph news on current events each, the former dealing with Hungary, the latter with foreign countries. Sample titles of recent articles: "55 Kilogram Per Capita Paper Consumption," "Hungarian Socialist Workers Party Stand on the 25th Congress of the Communist Party of the Soviet Union," "New Hungarian Films in 1976." 20 pages per issue. Published weekly at Hungarian News Agency MTI Publishing Office, P.O. Box 3, H-1426 Budapest, Hungary. $36.00 per year. (M) Since 1961.

Weekly Economic Report (see B.B.C. Monitoring Service).

Welcome to Czechoslovakia. Pictorial magazine. Articles on areas, monuments, cultural events, and other topics aimed at promoting tourism. Sample titles of recent articles: "Mountain Climbing in the High Tatra," "Summer Camps of the CKM [Youth Travel Agency]," "About the Houses of Prague." 64 pages per issue. Published quarterly by the CTK Press Agency for the Czech Government Committee for Tourism in Prague and the Slovak Government Committee for Tourism in Bratislava, Hastalska 14, 115 21 Prague 1, Czechoslovakia. (M) Since 1965.

Women of the Whole World. Pictorial magazine. Primary emphasis on the position and status of women in countries around the world and on the progress of women in their struggle for equal rights with men. Reports on international meetings. Sample titles of recent articles: "Democratic Republic of Vietnam: The Role of Women," "Peace Cannot Be Achieved without Women," "Women under Arab Legislation." Published quarterly by the Women's International Democratic Federation, Unter den Linden 13, 108 Berlin, German Democratic Republic. $2.50 per year. (M)

World Affairs Report. Highly critical analysis of Soviet news items, primarily from Pravda, with almost exclusive focus on Soviet foreign policy and Soviet relations with foreign countries. After a general section, items are classified on a region-by-region and a country-by-country basis. Usually no titles for individual articles. Around 105 to 110 pages per issue. Published quarterly at the California Institute of International Affairs, P.O. Box 4434, Stanford, California 94305. $6.00 per year. (N/M) Since 1973.

World Broadcasting Information (WBI) (see B.B.C. Monitoring Service).

World Markets. (see East-West Trade: World Markets).

World Marxist Review. Canadian edition of the Czechoslovak periodical Problems of Peace and Socialism. Articles relating to questions of ideology, political science, economics, culture, sociology, and international affairs; also analyses of events, conditions, and developments in socialist and nonsocialist countries. Book reviews; letters to the editor. Subscribers also receive, twice a month, Information Bulletin, described separately in this index. Sample titles of recent articles: "Socialism and the Technological Revolution," "The Strategic Aim of the Finnish Communists," "The Crisis of Capitalism and the Environment." Published monthly by Progress Books, 487 Adelaide Street West, Toronto, Ontario, Canada. 144 pages per issue. $5.00 per year; $9.00 for two years. (M) Since 1958.

World Student News. Illustrated magazine. Primary emphasis on ed-
    ucation and student activities around the world. Also articles on
    politics and economics of interest to Communist-oriented students.
    Sample titles of recent articles: "Higher Education and Students in
    Japan Today," "For the Democratization of the Irish Educational
    System by the Union of Students in Ireland," "Working People's
    Further Training and Education in the GDR." 24 pages per issue.
    Published monthly at 17th November Street, 110 01 Prague 01,
    Czechoslovakia. $5.00 per year. (M)

World Trade Union Movement. Articles on trade unions in countries
    around the globe. Sample titles of recent articles: "USSR: A New
    Type of Society Gives Rise to a New Type of Trade Unionism,"
    "Hungary: Give Greater Emphasis to the Goals of Socialism" "An-
    gola: Unions Stand Alongside the Revolutionary Forces." 32 pages
    per issue. Published monthly by W.F.T.U. (World Federation of
    Trade Unions) Publications Ltd., 103a Hoe Street, London E17
    4SA, England. $3.00 per year; $6.00 by airmail. (M)

Yearbook on International Communist Affairs. Surveys of Communist
    parties, both ruling and nonruling, of over 90 countries. Informa-
    tion on leadership changes, electoral strength, domestic and inter-
    national activities, ideological orientation, views on international
    issues, and so on. Analyses of major Communist international con-
    ferences and of 11 international organizations alleged to be Com-
    munist front organizations, such as the International Organization
    of Journalists, the International Union of Students, and the World
    Federation of Trade Unions. A "Checklist" gives for each of the
    countries covered the country's name, population, number of Com-
    munist party members, percentage of vote in last election, status
    (power, legal, and so on), and position in Sino-Soviet dispute (pro-
    Chinese, pro-Soviet, split, neutral, or independent). Biographical
    sketches of a few prominent Communist leaders (nine in the 1976
    edition). About 700 pages per issue. Published yearly by the
    Hoover Institution Press, Hoover Institution, Stanford, California
    94305. $25.00 per issue. (N/M) Since 1967.

Yivo Annual of Jewish Social Science. Primary concentration on four
    areas: (1) history and sociology of Ashkenazic Jewry, particularly
    in East Europe; (2) Yiddish folklore, literature, and linguistics,
    (3) impact of East Europe on American Jewish life; and (4) the
    Holocaust. Some articles deal specifically with communism. Sam-
    ple titles of recent articles: "The Attitude of the Communist Party
    of Russia to Jewish National Survival, 1918-1930," "The Russian

Jewish Labor Movement and Others." 300 to 330 pages per issue. Published twice a year by Yivo Institute for Jewish Research, 1048 Fifth Avenue, New York, N. Y. 10028. From $5.00 to $6.00 per volume. (N/M)

Young (Jeune) Cinema & Theatre. Illustrated magazine. Primary emphasis on film and theater; also articles on art and culture in general. Text in English and French. Sample titles of recent articles: "The Sense of Authenticity in Feature Films," "Art and National Liberation," "Some Aspects of UNESCO's Cultural Program." 48 pages per issue. Published quarterly by the International Union of Students, 17th November Street, P.O. Box 58, 110 01 Prague, Czechoslovakia. $3.00 per year. (M)

Youth Life (see Union of Yugoslav Youth. Newsletter).

Yugoslav Export. Illustrated periodical in newspaper format. Features reports on Yugoslav market conditions, opportunities for exports and imports, methods of doing business with Yugoslav companies, and other information of interest to Western investors. Sections on "Economic Relations," "News in Brief," "Fairs in Yugoslavia," "Yugoslavia at International Fairs," "New Products," "Tourism," "Banks," "Export-Import." Sample titles of recent articles: "The Five-Year Plan 1976-1980," "Yugoslav Business in the Far East," "Travel by Car Again in the Vogue." Eight pages per issue. Published monthly by Yugoslaviapublic, Publicity Office of the Yugoslav Chamber of Commerce, Knez Mihailova 10, P.O. Box 447, Belgrade, Yugoslavia. $10.00 per year. (M)

Yugoslav Facts and Views. Analyses of current events in Yugoslavia with primary emphasis on politics and economics. Speeches; documents. Usually entire issues devoted to one specific topic. Sample titles of recent issues: New Joint Ventures in Yugoslavia, The Federation in the New Constitution of the SFR of Yugoslavia, The Delegate System and the New Assembly Structure. Varying lengths, from four to more than twenty pages per issue. Published about once a month by the Yugoslav Press and Cultural Center, 488 Madison Avenue, New York, N. Y. 10022. Free. (M) Since 1974.

Yugoslav Governmental Pamphlets. Booklets dealing with economic and political conditions and developments in Yugoslavia and with Yugoslavia's economic, political, and social system. Each booklet devoted to one specific issue. Sample titles of recent booklets: The League of Communists of Yugoslavia in the System of Socialist Self-Management, Economic Development of Yugoslavia, Yugoslavia's Economic Relations with Foreign Countries. Averages about 60 pages per booklet. Published irregularly by the Secretariat for Information of the Federal Executive Council of Yugoslavia, Belgrade, Yugoslavia. Obtainable from the Yugoslav Press and Cultural Center, 488 Madison Avenue, New York, N. Y. 10022. Free. (M)

Yugoslav Information Bulletin. Articles, speeches, and documents, primarily on Yugoslavia's economic, political, and social conditions and developments and its relations with other countries. Sample titles of recent articles: "Self-Management Is One of the Laws of Socialist Development," "Dedication to the Policy of Non-alignment," "Thirtieth Anniversary of Independence of the DR of Viet Nam: Message of President Tito." About 30 pages per issue. Published monthly under the auspices of the League of Communists of Yugoslavia and the Socialist Alliance of Working People of Yugoslavia by Komunist, Socialist Thought and Practice, Trg Marksa i Engelsa 11, P.O. Box 233, 11000 Belgrade, Yugoslavia. Free. (M) Since 1974.

Yugoslav Life. Illustrated periodical in newspaper format concentrating on economic, political, social, cultural, and sports developments in Yugoslavia. "Cultural Chronicle." Letters to the editor. Sample titles of recent articles: "Belgrade: Thirty Years of Development in Peace," "Some Aspects of the Law on Foreign Capital Investment," "25th Anniversary of Dubrovnik Summer Festival: A Theatre Built through the Centuries." Eight pages per issue. Published monthly by Tanjug News Agency, Nemanjina 34, P.O. Box 609, 11001 Belgrade, Yugoslavia. $3.00 per year. (M) Since 1956.

Yugoslav News. News bulletin, focusing on Yugoslav economic, political, social, and cultural affairs. Usually each issue consists of one news item from the Tanjug News Agency. Occasionally articles are translated from other Yugoslav news sources. Sample titles of recent articles: "'Josip Broz Tito' School Opens in Kumrovec," "Yugoslavia's Participation in the 'Green Revolution,'" "U.S. Congressional Delegation Leaves Yugoslavia." Usually one page per issue. Published irregularly, about seven to ten times per month, by the Yugoslav Press and Cultural Center, 488 Madison Avenue, New York, N. Y. 10022. Free to editors of newspapers and magazines. Back issues may be requested by individuals. (M)

Yugoslav Survey. Articles on political, economic, social, and cultural developments in Yugoslavia. Sample titles of recent articles: "Non-agricultural Households—Available Resources, Expenditures, and Possession of Specific Durable Commodities in 1973," "Military Schools of the Yugoslav People's Army," "Relations between Yugoslavia and Japan." Averages 170 pages per issue. Published quarterly at Mose Pijade 8/I, P.O. Box 677, Belgrade, Yugoslavia. $14.00 per year. (M) Since 1960.

Yugoslav Tourist News and Commercial Information. Illustrated periodical. Emphasis on topics of interest to tourists and to businessmen wishing to establish commercial relations with Yugoslavia. Published monthly by Turisticka Stampa, Knez Mihajlova 21, Belgrade, Yugoslavia. $3.00 per year. (M) Since 1958.

Yugoslav Trade Unions. Articles mostly on economic and political issues. Primary emphasis on matters of direct interest to members of Yugoslavia's Confederation of Trade Unions. Sample titles of recent articles: "As He Manufactures and Creates Income, the Worker Plans and Decides as Well," "Strengthening Cooperation with Italian Trade Unions," "The End of the War in Vietnam: A Triumph of Mankind." 16 pages per issue. Published twice a month by the Confederation of Trade Unions of Yugoslavia, Trg Marks i Engelsa 5, Belgrade, Yugoslavia. 25 cents per issue. (M) Since 1960.

Yugoslavia Export-Import Directory. Publication useful for Western businessmen and women who want information about the Yugoslav market. Contains lists of export and import goods, Yugoslav trade enterprises, transport and forwarding enterprises, travel agencies, Yugoslav tourist offices abroad, international fairs and exhibitions in Yugoslavia, Yugoslav banks for international transactions, chambers of commerce (called "chambers of economy") in Yugoslavia, offices of the Yugoslav Federal Chamber of Economy abroad, and Yugoslav diplomatic representatives abroad. About 410 pages plus 70 pages of advertisements of goods Yugoslavia offers for sale abroad. Published yearly by Yugoslaviapublic, Knez Mihailova 10, P.O. Box 447, Belgrade, Yugoslavia. $5.00 per year. (M)

Periodicals originating in one of the socialist countries (for instance, China Pictorial), or published elsewhere but devoted to one of the socialist countries (for instance, China Quarterly), are listed under the respective country. Some are cross listed under "General," "Asia," or "East Europe" (see footnotes to these sections for further explanation); others, dealing specifically with two or more of the socialist countries (for instance, Poland and Germany), are cross listed under the respective countries.

(M) = Marxist material; (N/M) = non-Marxist material; (M; N/M) = Marxist and non-Marxist material; (U) = unclassified. For further explanation of these abbreviations, see page xi in the preface.

GENERAL*

ABN Correspondence (N/M)
ACES Bulletin (M; N/M)
African Communist (M)
AIMS Newsletter (M)
AIMS Publication Series (M; N/M)
American Review of East-West Trade (M; N/M)
B.B.C. Monitoring Service (M; N/M)
Communist Viewpoint (M)
Daily News Release (Hsinhua News Agency) (M)
Demographic Yearbook (M; N/M)
Directory of Trade (N/M)
East-West (Foreign Trade Board Report) (N/M)

---

*Includes periodicals dealing with Marxism or Marxism-Leninism in general, such as Political Affairs, and periodicals dealing with all or most of the socialist countries, such as Statistical Yearbook (United Nations). Periodicals that, for instance, deal with Marxist philosophy in general and also with one or more socialist countries specifically are cross listed.

East-West Commerce (U)
East-West Digest (N/M)
Economics of Planning (M; N/M)
Export Administration Report (N/M)
Foreign Affairs Research Papers Available (N/M)
Fourth International (M)
Information Bulletin (M)
International Affairs (Moscow) (M)
International Review of East-West Trade (N/M)
International Review of History and Political Science (N/M)
Journal of East and West Studies (N/M)
JPRS Reports (M; N/M)
Left Curve (M)
Marxism Today (M)
Marxist Studies (U)
Monthly Bulletin of Statistics (M; N/M)
Monthly Review (M)
Moscow Narodny Bank Limited: Quarterly Review (M)
New Times (M)
New World Review (M)
Northern Neighbors (M)
Orbis (N/M)
Political Affairs (M)
Problems of Communism (N/M)
Quarterly Economic Review (N/M)
RCDA—Religion in Communist Dominated Areas (M; N/M)
Religion in Communist Lands (N/M)
Review (Tokyo) (N/M)
Review of Socialist Law (M; N/M)
Science and Society (M)
Sport (M)
Statistical Yearbook (UNESCO) (M; N/M)
Statistical Yearbook (United Nations) (M; N/M)
Studies in Comparative Communism (N/M)
Studies on the Developing Countries (M)
Trends in Communist Media (N/M)
Trends in World Economy (M)
Twentieth Century and Peace (M)
U.S. Bureau of East-West Trade Office of Export Administration,
    Export Administration Report (N/M)
Women of the Whole World (M)
World Marxist Review (M)
World Student News (M)
World Trade Union Movement (M)

Yearbook of International Communist Affairs (N/M)
Young (Jeune) Cinema and Theatre (M)

ASIA*

Asia Letter (N/M)
Asia Quarterly (N/M)
Asian Affairs, an American Review (N/M)
Asian Outlook (N/M)
B.B.C. Monitoring Service (M; N/M)
Daily Report (Foreign Broadcast Information Service) (M; N/M)
Far East Reporter (N/M)
Far Eastern Affairs (M)
Far Eastern Economic Review (N/M)
Far Eastern Economic Review Yearbook (N/M)
Indochina Solidarity Committee, Newsletter (M)
Journal of Contemporary Asia (M; N/M)
JPRS Reports (M)
Pacific Community (N/M)
Problems of the Far East (M)
Quarterly Economic Review (N/M)
Statistical Yearbook for Asia and the Pacific (N/M)

EAST EUROPE†

AAASS Newsletter (N/M)
ABN Correspondence (N/M)
ABSEES (M; N/M)
ACES Bulletin (M; N/M)
American Bibliography of Slavic and East European Studies (N/M)

---

*Includes periodicals dealing with all or several of the socialist countries in Asia, that is, Cambodia, China, Laos, Mongolia, North Korea, the USSR, and Vietnam. Periodicals that deal with Asia in general and also with one or more of the socialist countries of Asia specifically are cross listed.
†Includes periodicals dealing with all or most of the socialist countries of East Europe, that is, Albania, Bulgaria, Czechoslovakia, German Democratic Republic, Hungary, Poland, Romania, the USSR, and Yugoslavia. Periodicals dealing with East Europe in general and also with one or more of the socialist countries of East Europe specifically are cross listed.

American Review of East-West Trade (M; N/M)
B.B.C. Monitoring Service (M; N/M)
Canadian American Slavic Studies (N/M)
Canadian Slavonic Papers (M; N/M)
Central Europe Journal (N/M)
Daily Report (Foreign Broadcast Information Service) (M; N/M)
East Central Europe (N/M)
East Europe (N/M)
East European Quarterly (M; N/M)
East European Trade (N/M)
East-West Fortnightly Bulletin (N/M)
East-West Market (N/M)
East-West Monthly Confidential Report (N/M)
East-West Research Reports (M; N/M)
East-West Trade: World Markets (N/M)
Eastern European Economics (M)
Economic Bulletin for Europe (M; N/M)
Economic Survey of Europe (M; N/M)
Florida State University Proceedings and Reports (N/M)
Foreign Affairs Research Papers Available (N/M)
Joint Economic Committee: Papers and Hearings (N/M)
JPRS Reports (M; N/M)
Labour in Exile (N/M)
Law in Eastern Europe (N/M)
Matekon (M)
New Review of East-European History (N/M)
Persecuted Church (N/M)
Quarterly Economic Review (N/M)
Radio Free Europe Research Publications on East European Affairs
    (M; N/M)
Review of Socialist Law (M; N/M)
RMASS Newsletter (N/M)
Selected Trade and Economic Data of the Centrally Planned Economies
    (N/M)
Slavic and Eastern European Journal (N/M)
Slavic Review (N/M)
Slavonic and East European Review (N/M)
Sociology and Eastern Europe (N/M)
Southeastern Europe (N/M)
Soviet and Eastern European Foreign Trade (M)
Soviet Jewish Affairs (N/M)
Soviet Studies (N/M)
Survey (N/M)
U.S. Trade Status with Socialist Countries (N/M)
Yivo Annual of Jewish Social Science (N/M)

ALBANIA

Albania Report (M)
Albania Today (M)
Albanian Resistance (M; N/M)
New Albania (M)
Quarterly Economic Review (N/M)
Southeastern Europe (N/M)

BULGARIA

Abstracts of Bulgarian Scientific Literature: Economics and Law (M)
BTA News Bulletin (M)
Bulgaria Today (M)
Bulgarian Films (M)
Bulgarian Foreign Trade (M)
Bulgarian Historical Review (M)
Bulgarian News and Views (M)
Bulgarian Studies Group Newsletter (N/M)
Bulgarian Trade Unions (M)
Economic News of Bulgaria (M)
Obzor (M)
Quarterly Economic Review (N/M)
Selected Trade and Economic Data of the Centrally Planned Economies
    (N/M)
Sofia News (M)
Southeastern Europe (N/M)

CAMBODIA

Far Eastern Economic Review Yearbook (N/M)
Indochina Solidarity Committee, Newsletter (M)
JPRS Reports (M)
Quarterly Economic Review (N/M)

CHINA

Asia Quarterly (N/M)
Asian Outlook (N/M)

B.B.C. Monitoring Service (M; N/M)
China and U.S. (N/M)
China Exchange Newsletter (N/M)
China Letter (N/M)
China News Analysis (N/M)
China Notes (N/M)
China Now (N/M)
China Pictorial (M)
China Policy Study Group Broadsheet (M)
China Quarterly (N/M)
China Reconstructs (M)
China Report (N/M)
China Trade and Economic Newsletter (N/M)
China Trade Report (M; N/M)
China Trade Telegram (U)
China's Foreign Trade (M)
Chinese Economic Studies (M; N/M)
Chinese Education (M)
Chinese Law and Government (M)
Chinese Literature (M)
Chinese Sociology and Anthropology (M)
Chinese Studies in History (M)
Chinese Studies in Philosophy (M)
CIA Office of Economic Research Aids (N/M)
Daily News Release (Hsinhua News Agency) (M)
Daily Report (Foreign Broadcast Information Service) (M; N/M)
East/West (N/M)
Eastern Horizon (M; N/M)
Economic Reporter: English Supplement (M)
Far East Reporter (N/M)
Far Eastern Economic Review Yearbook (N/M)
Foreign Affairs Research Papers Available (N/M)
Free China Review (N/M)
Hsinhua Weekly (M)
Issues and Studies (N/M)
Joint Economic Committee: Papers and Hearings (N/M)
Journal of East and West Studies (N/M)
JPRS Reports (M)
Modern China (N/M)
Modern China Series (M; N/M)
Modern China Studies: International Bulletin (N/M)
New China (N/M)
Peking Informers (N/M)
Peking Review (M)

CUBA

CZECHOSLOVAKIA

Kovoexport (M)
News Service (M)
Press Review (M)
Quarterly Economic Review (N/M)
Selected Trade and Economic Data of the Centrally Planned Economies
    (N/M)
Sport (M)
Statni Banka Ceskoslovenska (M)
Welcome to Czechoslovakia (M)
World Marxist Review (M)
World Student News (M)
Young (Jeune) Cinema and Theatre (M)

GERMAN DEMOCRATIC REPUBLIC

Foreign Affairs Bulletin (M)
GDR Review (M)
Poland and Germany (M; N/M)
Quarterly Economic Review (N/M)
Selected Trade and Economic Data of the Centrally Planned Economies
    (N/M)
Women of the Whole World (M)

HUNGARY

Abstracts of Hungarian Economic Literature (M)
Acta Historiae Artium (M)
Acta Historica (M)
Acta Litteraria (M)
Acta Oeconomica (M)
Booklets on Hungary (M)
Canadian-American Review of Hungarian Studies (N/M)
Daily News/Neueste Nachrichten (M)
Hungarian Agricultural Review (M)
Hungarian Book Review (M)
Hungarian Cooperation (M)
Hungarian Economy (M)
Hungarian Foreign Trade (M)
Hungarian Heavy Industries (M)
Hungarian Law Review (M)
Hungarian Music News (M)
Hungarian Musical Guide (M)

Hungarian Review (M)
Hungarian Studies Newsletter (N/M)
Hungarian Trade Union News (M)
Hungarian Travel Magazine (M)
Hungarofilm Bulletin (M)
Hungaropress Economic Information (M)
Hungary (M)
Interpressgrafik (M)
Marketing in Hungary (M)
New Hungarian Exporter (M)
New Hungarian Quarterly (M)
News from Hungary (M)
Press Summary (M)
Quarterly Economic Review (N/M)
Selected Trade and Economic Data of the Centrally Planned Economies
    (N/M)
Trends in World Economy (M)
Weekly Bulletin (M)

LAOS

Far Eastern Economic Review Yearbook (N/M)
Indochina Solidarity Committee Newsletter (M)
JPRS Reports (M)
Quarterly Economic Review (N/M)

MONGOLIA

East-West Fortnightly Bulletin (N/M)
East-West Monthly Confidential Report (N/M)
Far Eastern Economic Review Yearbook (N/M)
JPRS Reports (M)
Mongolian Studies (N/M)
Quarterly Economic Review (N/M)
U.S. Trade Status with Socialist Countries (N/M)

NORTH KOREA

Democratic People's Republic of Korea (M)
East Asian Review (N/M)
Far Eastern Economic Review Yearbook (N/M)

Journal of East and West Studies (N/M)
Journal of Korean Affairs (M; N/M)
JPRS Reports (M)
Korea Focus (N/M)
Korea Today (M)
Pyongyang Times (M)
Quarterly Economic Review (N/M)

POLAND

Acta Poloniae Historica (M)
Contemporary Poland (M)
Dialectics and Humanism (M)
Holidays in Poland (M)
Narodowy Bank Polski: Information Bulletin (M)
New Polish Publications (M)
Poland (M)
Poland and Germany (M; N/M)
Poland Tourism (M)
Polish Affairs (U)
Polish Art Review (M)
Polish Co-operative Review (M)
Polish Economic Survey (M)
Polish Facts and Figures (M)
Polish Fair Magazine (M)
Polish Film/Film Polonais (M)
Polish Foreign Trade (M)
Polish Literature/Littérature Polonaise (M)
Polish Maritime News (M)
Polish Music/Polnische Musik (M)
Polish News Bulletin of the American and British Embassies (M)
Polish Perspectives (M)
Polish Review (N/M)
Polish Sociological Bulletin (M)
Polish Weekly (M)
Polish Western Affairs (M)
Quarterly Economic Review (N/M)
Quarterly of the Polish Western Association of America (N/M)
Selected Trade and Economic Data of the Centrally Planned Economies
    (N/M)
Studies on the Developing Countries (M)
Théâtre en Pologne/Theatre in Poland (M)

ROMANIA

USSR

Culture and Life (M)
Current Digest of the Soviet Press (M)
Daily Report (Foreign Broadcast Information Service) (M; N/M)
Daily Review (M)
Digest of the Soviet Ukranian Press (M)
East Europe (N/M)
East-West Fortnightly Bulletin (N/M)
East-West Market (N/M)
East-West Monthly Confidential Report (N/M)
East-West Research Reports (M; N/M)
East-West Trade: World Markets (N/M)
Economic Bulletin for Europe (M; N/M)
Economic Survey of Europe (M; N/M)
Ecotass (M)
Elta Bulletin (N/M)
Far Eastern Affairs (M)
Foreign Affairs Research Papers Available (N/M)
Foreign Trade (M)
In Soviet Ukraine (M)
Index to Pravda (M; N/M)
Information Moscow (M)
Insight: Soviet Jews (N/M)
International Affairs (Moscow) (M)
Jews and the Jewish People (M)
Jews in the USSR (N/M)
Joint Economic Committee: Papers and Hearings (N/M)
Journal of the Moscow Patriarchate (M)
Journal of the US–USSR Trade and Economic Council (N/M)
JPRS Reports (M)
Latvian Information Bulletin (N/M)
Law in Eastern Europe (N/M)
Lithuania Today (M)
Lituanus (N/M)
Matekon (M)
Moscow Narodny Bank Limited: Quarterly Review (M)
Moscow News (M)
New Times (M)
News Bulletin (M)
News from Ukraine (M)
Newsletter from behind the Iron Curtain (N/M)
Northern Neighbors (M)
Persecuted Church (N/M)
Problems of Economics (M)
Problems of the Contemporary World (M)

Soviet Union (University of Pittsburgh) (N/M)
Soviet Weekly (M)
Soviet World Outlook (N/M)
Soviet Woman (M)
Sport in the USSR (M)
Sputnik (M)
Sputnik Junior (M)
Studies in Soviet Thought (N/M)
Survey (N/M)
Travel to the USSR (M)
Twentieth Century and Peace (M)
Ukraine (M)
Ukranian Quarterly (N/M)
Ukranian Review (London) (N/M)
Ukranian Review (New York) (N/M)
U.S. Trade Status with Socialist Countries (N/M)
USSR and the Third World (M; N/M)
World Affairs Report (N/M)
Yivo Annual of Jewish Social Science (N/M)

VIETNAM

China News Analysis (N/M)
Far Eastern Economic Review Yearbook (N/M)
Giai Phong (M)
Indochina Solidarity Committee, Newsletter (M)
JPRS Reports (M; N/M)
Quarterly Economic Review (N/M)
Vietnam (M)
Vietnam Courier (M)
Vietnam Youth (M)
Vietnamese Trade Unions Review (M)

YUGOSLAVIA

Bridge (M)
Croatia Press (N/M)
Democratic Journalist (M)
East-West Fortnightly Bulletin (N/M)
East-West Monthly Confidential Report (N/M)
Economic Echo from Yugoslavia (M)
Economic Review (M)

Export Journal (M)
Florida State University Proceedings and Reports (N/M)
Index (M)
Journal of Croatian Studies (M; N/M)
Journal of Yugoslav Foreign Trade (M)
Jugoslawische Touristenzeitung/Yugoslav Tourist News (M)
New Yugoslav Law (M)
OECD Economic Survey (N/M)
OECD Foreign Trade Statistics (N/M)
Quarterly Economic Review (N/M)
Review (Belgrade) (M)
Review (London) (N/M)
Review of International Affairs (M)
Socialist Thought and Practice (M)
Southeastern Europe (N/M)
Studies and Documents (M)
Tanjug Features (M)
Translation Service (M)
Union of Yugoslav Youth. Newsletter (M)
Yugoslav Export (M)
Yugoslav Export-Import Directory (M)
Yugoslav Facts and Views (M)
Yugoslav Governmental Pamphlets
Yugoslav Information Bulletin (M)
Yugoslav Life (M)
Yugoslav News (M)
Yugoslav Survey (M)
Yugoslav Tourist News and Commercial Information (M)
Yugoslav Trade Unions (M)

SELECTED BOOK STORES AND AGENCIES IN THE UNITED STATES HANDLING SUBSCRIPTIONS TO PERIODICALS PUBLISHED IN SOCIALIST COUNTRIES

There are many organizations in cities throughout the United States that accept subscriptions to periodicals published in one or more of the socialist countries. The partial list below consists of some of the best-known organizations, many of them book stores, and the official agents of book and periodical distribution centers of socialist countries that are most often listed in these countries' periodicals and announcements.

Name	Address	Areas of specialization
Albania Report	P.O. Box 913 New York, N.Y. 10008	Albania (primarily for two periodicals, Albania Report and Albania Today)
Book Center	518 Valencia Street San Francisco, California 94110	Soviet Union, East Europe, Vietnam, North Korea, Cuba
China Books & Periodicals	2929 24th Street San Francisco, California 94110	China, Vietnam
	125 Fifth Avenue New York, N.Y. 10003	
	210 West Madison Street Chicago, Illinois 60606	
EBSCO Subscription Services	P.O. Box 1943 Birmingham, Alabama 35201 (branches in many U.S. cities—write for list)	All socialist countries

---

Note that two of the organizations listed are not in the United States, namely the Peace Book Company in Hong Kong (handling periodicals from China and Vietnam) and Progress Books in Canada (handling periodicals from the USSR). These two are official agents for Guozi Shudian, Peking, and for Mezhdurodnaya Kniga, Moscow, respectively. They are included here because I have found them to be extremely reliable and prompt in answering inquiries.

132

Name	Address	Areas of specialization
European Publishers Representatives	11-03 46th Avenue Long Island City, N.Y. 11101	Poland, Hungary
Fam Book Service	69 Fifth Avenue New York, N.Y. 10003	All socialist countries in Europe
Four Continents Book Corporation	149 Fifth Avenue New York, N.Y. 10010	USSR
Hungarian Books and Records	11802 Buckeye Road Cleveland, Ohio 44120	Hungary
Imported Publications	320 West Ohio Street Chicago, Illinois 60610	USSR, Bulgaria, Czechoslovakia, GDR, Hungary, Poland
May 1st Bookstore (formerly Long March)	2706 1/2 West 7th Street Los Angeles, California 90057	China
Peace Book Company	Chung Shang Building 7/F 9-10 Queen Victoria Street Hong Kong	China, Vietnam
People's Book Store Ksiegarnia Ludowa	5347 Chene Street Detroit, Michigan 48211	Poland
Polish Publication Center, Imported Books and Magazines	2917 North Central Park Avenue Chicago, Illinois 60618	Poland
Polonia Bookstore and Publishers Company	2921 North Milwaukee Avenue Chicago, Illinois 60618	Poland
Progress Books	487 Adelaide Street West Toronto 2 B, Ontario Canada	USSR
Progressive Book Store	1506 West 7th Street Los Angeles, California 90017	GDR
Romanian Library	866 Second Avenue New York, N.Y. 10017	Romania (distributes free of charge Romanian Bulletin; will furnish information on others)
UCIS and East European Publications	University Center for International Studies University of Pittsburgh G-6 Mervis Hall Pittsburgh, Pennsylvania 15260	Bulgaria, GDR, Hungary, Romania, Yugoslavia

Name	Address	Areas of specialization
Universal Book Store	52-4 West 13th Street New York, N.Y. 10003	All socialist countries
Yugoslav Press and Cultural Center	488 Madison Avenue New York, N.Y. 10022	Yugoslavia (distributes some periodicals free; will furnish information on others)

ABOUT THE AUTHOR

HARRY G. SHAFFER is Professor of Economics and Slavic and
Soviet Area Studies at the University of Kansas. A New York University Ph.D., he has visited and carried out extensive interviews in the
Soviet Union and all the socialist countries of East Europe except Albania.

Dr. Shaffer has published widely in the field of Slavic and Soviet
Area Studies. He has to his credit six books and more than 40 arti-
cles and book reviews which have been published or reprinted in seven
languages in such journals as The American Economic Review, The
Journal of Industrial Economics, The Journal of Higher Education,
The Slavic Review, Problems of Communism, The Russian Review,
East Europe, Osteuropa, Osteuropa Wirtschaft, Revue de l'Est, The
Antioch Review, Soviet and Eastern European Foreign Trade, The
Kansas Business Review and Queen's Quarterly. He has given papers
and lectures at numerous professional conferences and at universities
in the United States, Canada, and Germany.

CURRENT RESEARCH IN COMPARATIVE
COMMUNISM: An Analysis and Bibliographic
Guide to the Soviet System

Lawrence L. Whetten

SOVIET ASIA—BIBLIOGRAPHIES: A Com-
pilation of Social Sciences and Humanities
Sources on the Iranian, Mongolian, and
Turkic Nationalities

Edward Allworth

INPUT-OUTPUT ANALYSIS AND THE
SOVIET ECONOMY: An Annotated Bibliography

Vladimir G. Treml

SOVIET SOCIOLOGY, 1964-1975

T. Anthony Jones and
Mervyn Mathews